EXPATRIATES OF NO COUNTRY

EXPATRIATES OF NO COUNTRY

THE LETTERS OF SHIRLEY HAZZARD AND DONALD KEENE

EDITED BY

BRIGITTA OLUBAS

Columbia University Press   *New York*

Columbia University Press
Publishers Since 1893
New York   Chichester, West Sussex

Library of Congress Cataloging-in-Publication Data
Names: Hazzard, Shirley, 1931–2016, author. | Keene, Donald, author.
| Olubas, Brigitta, editor.
Title: Expatriates of no country : the letters of Shirley Hazzard and
Donald Keene / Shirley Hazzard and Donald Keene ;
edited by Brigitta Olubas.
Description: New York : Columbia University Press, 2024. | Includes
bibliographic references and index.
Identifiers: LCCN 2024022410 | ISBN 9780231214445 (hardback) |
ISBN 9780231214452 (trade paperback) | ISBN 9780231560344 (ebook)
Subjects: LCSH: Hazzard, Shirley, 1931–2016—Correspondence. |
Keene, Donald—Correspondence. | LCGFT: Personal
correspondence.
Classification: LCC PR9619.3.H369 Z48 2024 |
DDC 823/.914—dc23/eng/20240626

Cover design: Julia Kushnirsky

CONTENTS

EXPATRIATES
OF NO
COUNTRY

INTRODUCTION

This book tells the story of a friendship between two extraordinary writers, Shirley Hazzard and Donald Keene, through their correspondence. They were brought together by the death of a mutual friend. Ivan Morris was, like Keene, a scholar of Japanese literature. He died suddenly and prematurely in 1977; a memorial for him provided the occasion for their meeting and for the thirty-year correspondence that followed. With his first letter, Keene sent Hazzard one of the obituaries he had written for Morris, a beautiful admixture of affection and professional admiration, offering praise for Morris's eccentricity and his erudition alongside his own sense of personal loss. The qualities Keene singles out for remembrance offer a window onto values he shared also with Hazzard. They give a sense of what brought them together in a friendship of mutual admiration and unashamed embrace of learning and high culture, beauty, arcana, accomplishment. He wrote:

[Morris's] English was that of a virtuoso: the translation, into an idiom reminiscent of Defoe, of Saikaku's *The Life of an Amorous Woman* is nothing short of dazzling. He told me once that he had verified the usage by the eighteenth century of every word in that translation. No doubt it was tedious looking up all the words, but it was typical of him not to spare the effort, and it made the translation uniquely effective.[1]

A few years later, Keene sent Hazzard a copy of *Meeting with Japan*, a collection of articles he had been commissioned to write for the newspaper *Tōkyō Shimbun* on the subject of "what Japan has meant to me."[2] In her reply, she drew on his understanding of his complex location in Japan to express her own relation to Italy, where she lived for part of each year:

> I remember your saying—writing—in your "Meeting with Japan" that you came to depend on Japan for your happiness and thus to be sure that Japan could console you also for unhappiness. There are many for whom such a place does not exist even in fancy, and part of my own conscious joy in merely being in "my" chosen land is the sense of luck that Flaubert describes on the Nile: of gratitude that one is able to realise all this and look on with that awareness. I think that you, like me, came to this after you were quite grown up, and having enjoyed other places meantime, though not with this particular calm exultation. In my case, the sense of place was scarcely existent in childhood, and was perhaps saved up for the intensified adult pleasure later on.[3]

Both spoke of their "chosen land" in terms of great devotion: "The only way to describe my relationship to the city of Kyoto is to say it was love at first sight."[4] "When I entered [Naples] I knew that it was a *coup de foudre*. I knew that this was where I wanted to be. I became joyful . . . really for the first time I knew what joy was. It became a part of my life, I understood at last what that was."[5] Their friendship traced the tenuous lines of expatriate connection; serendipitous, passionate, often solitary.

Both had made substantial lives away from their country of birth. Keene had spent the war learning Japanese in the U.S. Navy and was stationed for a time in Japan. His postwar years were taken up with further study of the language at Columbia, Harvard, and Cambridge and in Japan. From the 1970s, he taught the spring term at Columbia University and spent much of the rest of the year in Tokyo. He was an inveterate traveler, adding destinations to lecture tours late into his life and giving talks on ocean cruises. Hazzard left her native Australia very young and made only a handful of short return visits. From the 1970s, she divided her time between Italy and New York. This displacement, as much as their intellectual and literary engagements and accomplishments, defined the life and career of both.

Shirley Hazzard died in 2016, aged eighty-five, an acclaimed novelist, winner of the National Book Award and of Australia's most prestigious literary prize, the Miles Franklin Award, for her final novel, *The Great Fire* (2003), and of the National Book Critics' Circle Award for her masterpiece, *The Transit of Venus* (1980); *The Bay of Noon* was a finalist for the 1970 Lost Man Booker Prize. Her writing is admired for its self-reflective delicacy of phrasing, its wit and irony, its intensely personal resonance, and its finely realized sense of place. She is one of the great writers of movement, passage, and transit. Her novels delineate a writerly sensibility that finds its location, as well as its most receptive audience, unconfined by national borders and paradigms. They trace the fates of young expatriate women within the geographical and emotional worlds opening up after World War II but before the social upheavals of feminism, and take her readers into moral territory that is at once utterly sure and breached at every turn, where the certainties of romance forms are tested by human vulnerability and the often brutal social and political canvas of modern life.

In all her writing, Hazzard crafted a wholeheartedly cosmopolitan perspective, insisting that "my temperament is not a very national one,"[6] that "it is a privilege—to be at home in more than one place," and refuting the designation "expatriate": "I'm not even sure which country I'd be an expatriate of."[7] In place of the nation, Hazzard directs readers to the broad web of humanist inheritance. In her understanding of the work of culture and its place in the world, humanism provides an intellectual and imaginative bedrock. It signals the larger interconnections that make meaning of individual endeavors. It marks the work both of reading and writing, of attending to occluded as well as vaunted moments and objects, and it provides for unexpected points of recognition and understanding: "Humanism set the dignity and singularity of a man or woman above abstractions and inventions. Through generations of the world's fratricidal convulsions, it supplied the fragile continuity of individual civilization. It offered hospitality to thought and art."[8] In her novels, she invokes humanism's principles through the dense morality that underscores their intricate plotting, and in her striking use of literary allusion or oblique quotation. These qualities combine to create novels of great stylistic elegance and narrative density through which deeply familiar narratives of love, loss, and aspiration play out.

The writer Jay Parini drew attention to what he called the "sweep" of Hazzard's fiction, the "global view" that it provides of the world of its readers and protagonists and its traversal of "the entire world," a narrative passage that "manages to alight everywhere."[9] Within this global reach, Hazzard's fictional worlds are those of the postwar, carved out in the wake, above all, of Hiroshima, which she had visited, aged sixteen, in 1947. The ramifications of the cataclysm are found through her work; they define the moral scope of her protagonists' lives. Michael Hofmann observed that she would have "desired, as a novelist and as a woman, to make amends, to heal the atom by recombining her particulate characters in the right way . . . to find some better future for the species," adding, "You could say the whole purpose of Hazzard's enterprise, in life and fiction, was to put the world together again, and do it properly (and by the rules of art and love and goodness)." Further, "[i]n some fairly real way, the protagonists of her books are the continents of this blasted planet, and what she is doing is hauling Australia . . . up to Asia."[10]

Hazzard's four novels are set in the decades through which she lived and are marked by the great cadences of the twentieth century. She wrote to a friend, "What has attracted me—even, perhaps pleased me—is to look at, live, trace this strange caper of modern life in the constant presence and awareness of poverty and war . . . the endless 'music' of the two world wars and the Depression that haunts a life-span like mine."[11] She had left Sydney aged sixteen; had lived with her family in Hong Kong and Wellington, New Zealand; then in 1952, still with her family, traveled to New York, where she worked as a stenographer at the United Nations. Fiercely intelligent and instinctively intellectual, she embarked on a project of self-education through extensive and passionate reading and through friendships with the literary elite of New York.

Her marriage to the translator and biographer Francis Steegmuller was marked throughout by the couple's commitment to literary amateurism and belles lettres, traditions marked, as Timothy Duffy has observed, by idiosyncrasy and individuality.[12] Steegmuller was a private scholar; his research and writing were supported in part by writing commissions, publishing advances, and the like, but primarily by the income bequeathed to him by his wealthy first wife, Beatrice Stein Steegmuller, a talented amateur painter and philanthropist. Hazzard, too, had been living off her writing for a year or two when she met Steegmuller in 1963, thanks to the generous (absurdly so, from the perspective of the present day) First Writing Agreement offered by *The New Yorker* magazine. She had also begun spending time regularly in Italy as well as New York after having been posted for a year to Naples in 1956. Her marriage consolidated this pattern: writing, reading and traveling, and spending time in stimulating conversation with the literary elites around them. The Steegmullers rented apartments in Naples, Capri, and the Upper East Side of Manhattan and moved between them through the year in well-trodden patterns: spring and autumn in Italy, August and December in New York. They read and reread, above all, the European canon; by way of example, Hazzard gave this list of works they read aloud together in the last decade of Steegmuller's life: "Shakespeare, Gibbon, Byron's 'Don Juan,' Clough's 'Amours de Voyage,' Thucydides, Seneca, Auden, Delacroix's journals, Leopardi's 'Canti.'"[13] If such a writerly habitus is today no longer really imaginable, it was already unusual, even remarkable, in the immediate postwar decades.

While Steegmuller's erudition and scholarship were grounded in his prewar years at Columbia, Hazzard had not even completed high school. There was a certain anachronism, and an unlocatedness, in her intellectual bearing; an autodidact who had made her way into the cultural life of New York from the far reaches of the colonial netherworld, pursuing intellectual modes that were already being relegated to the past. She had always operated to a degree outside the circuits of contemporary cultural life. To describe Hazzard and Steegmuller as amateur writers is to highlight not a lesser achievement or, as Roland Barthes has it, "a lesser knowledge, an imperfect technique," but rather to assert the centrality of devotion in their pursuit of a life of letters. Amateurism is found, Barthes writes, "simultaneously at the highest and the lowest level: as Arcanum of enjoyment and as a modest hobby not to be exhibited," a domain of pleasure not defined by a paying public. The amateur seeks "to produce only his own enjoyment"; he is "the one who does not make himself heard."[14]

Donald Keene died in 2019 at age ninety-six, an acclaimed scholar of Japanese literature who had published more than twenty books in English and another thirty or so in Japanese, translations, literary histories, or monographs on individual authors, covering all major periods, from the eighth to the twentieth centuries. Keene was revered in Japan for his scholarship and his devotion to Japanese language and culture. His fellow Japanologist Carol Gluck observed that he was "almost the most famous man in Japan . . . You can't go anywhere in Japan and utter the words 'Donald Keene' and not have everybody know him."[15] One of his former students, the Japanese American journalist Fred Katayama, observed that in Japan, Keene was seen as the foreigner who best knew and understood the country and the people.[16] Keene received many of the most prestigious Japanese literary awards, including the Kikuchi Kan Prize (1962), the Yamagata Bantō Prize (1983), the Japan Foundation Prize (1982), the Asahi Prize (1990), and the Inoue Yasushi Prize (1994), and was the first non-Japanese to receive the Yomiuri Prize for *Hyakudai no Kakyaku*, the Japanese original later published in English as *Travelers of a Hundred Ages* (1989). He was also awarded the National Book Critics Circle Ivan Sandorf Award (1991) in the United States. Further Japanese honors included the Order of the Rising Sun in 1975 and 1993, and he was the first non-Japanese to receive the Order of Culture, conferred by the emperor in 2008.

Notwithstanding Keene's extraordinary productivity and his employment at Cambridge and Columbia universities, there was a dimension of Barthes's amateur in his career as a scholar from the start, above all in his devotion to Japanese language and literature but also in the extraordinary range and scope of his writing and teaching, for instance, the "unattainable" goal he had set himself of "learning everything about Japan"[17] and the fact that he had been, as he wrote, for many years "the only person to teach Japanese literature at Columbia" and so had had to "cover all periods."[18] This capacious approach was evident from the start in his prodigious enthusiasm both for learning the language and for disseminating that knowledge to the widest possible audience. On his first military posting to Honolulu in 1943, he arranged for his one day off each week to be spent studying Japanese literature at the University of Hawaii. "The first term we read a modern novel each week, and wrote a report in Japanese. I had never before read anything in Japanese as long as a novel, and it was exhilarating to discover I could do it."[19] He reflected on his 1955 *Anthology of Japanese Literature*—which quickly sold out its first printing of two thousand copies and has remained in print ever since: "Its success brought home to me again . . . that I was really not cut out to be a scholar who produces one perfect research article every decade and that my greatest strength lay in communicating to other people the excitement I felt on reading works of Japanese literature."[20]

Keene's study of Japanese language and literature had its roots in his passionate opposition to war. At the age of eighteen, troubled by the progress of the war in Europe, he had come across a translation of the eleventh-century Japanese novel *The Tale of Genji*. He returned often in interviews and in memoirs to the importance of this moment. During the German bombing of Britain, he had been overcome with despair, and the novel offered "a kind of deliverance" to him in the world it conjured:

The translation (by Arthur Waley) was magical, evoking a distant and beautiful world. I could not stop reading, sometimes going back to savor the details again. I contrasted the world of *The Tale of Genji* with my own. In the book, antagonism never degenerated into violence, and there were no wars. The hero, Genji, unlike the heroes of European epics, was not described as a man of muscle, capable of lifting a boulder that not ten men could lift, or as a warrior who could single-handedly slay masses of the enemy. Nor, though he had many love affairs, was Genji interested (like Don Juan) merely in adding names to the list of women he had conquered. He knew grief, not because he had failed to seize the government, but because he was a human being and life in this world is inevitably sad.[21]

So Keene, a pacifist, enrolled in the U.S. Navy in order to learn Japanese. His first assignment, in 1943, was to interrogate Japanese prisoners of war at Pearl Harbor and to translate related documents. Uninspired by the inconsequential nature of the translations he worked on, he happened upon "a box filled with malodorous little books" seized during the campaign on Guadalcanal, in the Solomon Islands, that turned out to be "diaries taken from the bodies of dead Japanese soldiers and sailors. The odor was caused by the dried blood with which many of these diaries were stained." The diaries, which became his "special field of competence" during his time in the navy, were difficult to read because they were handwritten and because "the diary, unlike the printed or mimeographed documents I previously had translated, was at times almost unbearably moving, recording the suffering of a soldier in his last days."[22]

He was repeatedly struck by the distance he felt between himself and some of his fellow Americans, who seemed to have only one wish, "to return to their former lives,"[23] in contrast to the sense of friendship that developed with some of the Japanese ("I discovered these people had read the same books that I had"[24]). This contrast "haunted" him, he wrote, adding nuance to his thinking about war, defeat, and victory: "the consecration of the Japanese to their cause," on the one hand, and "the total indifference of most Americans to anything except returning home." He added, "Although I did not in the least accept the ideals of the Japanese militarists, I could not help but feel admiration for the ordinary Japanese soldiers, and in the end I came to believe that the Japanese really deserved to win the war."[25] He wrote movingly, in an essay in 1946, of his friendship with one prisoner, the naval officer Sato, with whom he discussed "the great books of the West as well as the East. He was ready to discuss Greek tragedy or philosophy, but equally the works of Proust and Joyce."[26] He decided one evening to bring his phonograph to the camp to play a recording of Beethoven's Third symphony because he knew this would bring pleasure to Sato. His account of the evening, playing the records in the shower room (for the acoustics), details the responses of one after another of the prisoners: one a former taxi driver, another a former news reporter, another a former doctor. "Nothing stood between us. If on no other ground, we could meet on that of music. The music was as true for them as for me, in spite of our different backgrounds, in spite of the cement and concrete shower room."[27]

In his scholarship, Keene was interested above all in figures of transposition and mobility in the world, and in pivots of change; figures devoted to the discovery of otherness, or new worlds and perspectives. This led him to write biographies of, for instance, the Emperor Meiji, whose rule saw Japan's opening to the West, its dramatic change in the mid-nineteenth century from feudal country into "not only a world power but also a member of the community of nations,"[28] and of the fifteenth-century shogun Yoshimasa, whom Keene describes as possibly "the worst shogun ever to rule Japan,"[29] who after a disastrous reign resigned from his post, withdrew to a retreat he had had built, which later became Ginkaku-ji, Temple of the Silver Pavilion, where he devoted his time to aesthetic pursuits, and played a decisive role in the development of what is today understood as Japanese taste, or "soul (*kokoro*) of Japan, the aesthetic preferences of the Japanese,"[30] across all the arts from nō theater to the tea ceremony; to poetry, architecture, and painting.

Keene was drawn to the ways that traditional forms were reworked in later contexts; indeed this was the focus of a Ford Foundation Fellowship he was granted in 1953 to study "the survival of classical literary traditions in contemporary Japan."[31] He found an exemplary instance of this in Mishima Yukio's nō works, which Keene translated, describing them as "[t]he first genuinely successful modern Nō plays."[32] In both his personal and professional lives—it is impossible really to separate the two, so wholehearted was his pursuit of learning—Keene labored to glean a view from outside, a view not yet granted to others, and then to share that view with as wide a public as possible. In 1952, he published *The Japanese Discovery of Europe*, about a group of Japanese, called "rangakusha," who devoted themselves during the period of Japan's closure to the world to learning about the West, including European languages, and thus picking up vital scientific knowledge and expertise that Japan lacked. They acquired books and materials from a group of Dutch merchants, at that time "[t]he only Europeans permitted to reside in Japan," living on an island in Nagasaki Bay. He saw himself in one of these rangakusha, Honda Toshiaki, "a man who was in a sense my opposite number."

Unlike Honda Toshiaki, I had turned to Japan—not for the sake
of my country or for technical knowledge that might benefit my
countrymen, but for the pleasure of new knowledge. It was difficult to learn the many characters used in writing Japanese, and
there were always problems in guessing the correct pronunciations
of the names of people and places, but this was part of the appeal
of Japanese. . . . [I]t was only by comparing my problems with
those Honda Toshiaki and the other scholars of Dutch learning
had faced at a time when there were no dictionaries or grammars
to help them that I was able to see myself in a somewhat better
perspective. I too, like Honda Toshiaki the rangakusha, wanted to
discover another civilization.[33]

Keene was always very clear that in his scholarship he wished
to emulate older forms of erudition and learning, to keep alive
pedagogical traditions that had moved and excited him as a
student. He wrote of several mentors on whom he modeled his
own approach and career; most of all two of his earliest Columbia teachers, Mark van Doren who showed Keene "that praising
another is the most specifically human of actions,"[34] and Tsunoda
Ryūsaku, who, Keene wrote, "read literature widely and loved it,
but he did not think of it as a subject of academic research."[35]
Central, too, were two of his Harvard teachers, Edwin Reischauer
and William Hung. Reischauer, Keene observed, wrote unapolo-
getically "for the general public rather than for specialists" because
of the immense ignorance about Japan in the United States in the
pre- and postwar years. He was "the best exemplar I have known
of a scholarly ideal, belonging to more than one country."[36] Hung
taught a course Keene took on the Chinese poet Tu Fung.

Doctor Hung could not have been better prepared to give this
course. He had read everything written about Tu Fu in English,

German, and Japanese, in addition to (of course) Chinese. He knew most of the poems by heart. One day he recited one of the long poems, not in standard Chinese but in the Fukien dialect, which was his own. I can still see him, leaning back, his eyes shut, reciting words that were a part of his body and soul. The rhymes that have disappeared from standard Chinese can still be heard when recited in Fukien dialect, with the crack of the final consonants. At the end I saw the tears in his eyes. This, I thought, was the kind of scholarship I wanted to practice.[37]

Keene was himself a remarkable teacher. He taught with great formality and without notes, his students recalled. "His lectures are all in his head, and he is extremely passionate. You can feel it in the tenor of his voice, his mannerisms, the way he holds himself. There's a Japanese sensibility to him—modest, quiet, extremely diligent, but never patronising or condescending."[38] Keene's scholarly passion communicated itself to his students just as to his readers, as Carol Gluck observed: "You don't feel like it's a kind of knowledge. His generosity and spirit, combined with his delight in Japanese literature, generates affection even in people who are very shy and think he's a great man. There's no space between him as a teacher and his subject, and you as students."[39]

Keene's early work translating prisoners' diaries reverberated across his later writing and thinking, defining, in a way, its tone and interest, his place as a scholar. In 1982, he was invited by the newspaper *Asahi Shimbun* to write a series of essays (five each week for two years, later published in two volumes, first in Japanese and later in English[40]) on Japanese diaries from the eighth century to the twentieth. The pace of writing for initial serial publication was, Keene wrote, "hectic" and, as one reviewer observed, "Only someone who has immersed himself in the great pool of Japanese diary literature could have maintained such a gruelling pace."[41] In 2010, aged nearly ninety, he published another study, this time focused on the diaries of Japanese writers during the years of the Pacific War. This book brought together his interest in the diary form, with its combination of personal and public expression and commemoration, the meeting of art and politics and humanity and brutality that had preoccupied him during his wartime period in Japan; his complex responses, as an avowed pacifist, to Japanese militarism, together with his sympathies with individual soldiers.

He had known several of the writers—had translated and written about their work—and found their diaries sometimes surprising: "The diary of Itō Sei (1905–1969) . . . came as a shock. The person revealed in its pages, especially those written just after the outbreak of war, did not in the least resemble the soft-spoken, humorous, kindly man I had known."[42] And more so:

> Reading the diary of Yamada Fūtarō (1922–2001) proved I was wrong in supposing that the books one reads form one's character and beliefs. He and I had read, at about the same times, the same books, yet our outlooks on the world were radically different. Tamada intensely desired a Japanese victory and refused to consider that the war might end with anything but a victory. Even after witnessing the bombing of Tokyo, he did not waver in his conviction that Japan must never surrender.[43]

But he found, also, moments of deeply shared experience, particularly with the diaries of the poet and novelist Takami Jun, who was careful never to "openly express antipathy for the militarism that dominated Japan," but who "desperately hoped for an end to the war, even if (though he did not write this in so many words) it was in defeat."[44] Keene was particularly drawn to one passage from Takami's diary, from March 1945 in the wake of U.S. air raids on Tokyo. Takami decided to send his mother to the country for safety and had gone with her to Ueno Station, which was crowded with others also fleeing. He was struck by the great civility of this crowd: "Everybody is quiet, everybody's just moving slowly and no one is trying to get ahead of anyone else."[45] Takami was deeply moved by this experience, and Keene quotes his account: "Before I knew it, tears had poured from my eyes. My heart was full of love and affection. I thought that I wanted to live with these people and die with them. No—though I was not the victim of a bombing, I was one with such people. These ordinary people have not been authorized to emit angry voices. They have no influence they can depend on, no money, but as they wait in patient silence they love and trust Japan from their hearts. I was one with them."[46]

Keene was struck by the ethos of human fragility and community; it helped frame for him a final significant decision, late in life in 2011, to give up his U.S. citizenship and move to Tokyo. He had been very ill in a Japanese hospital and thought he might die. And recalling Takami's words about his mother at Ueno, thought, "What would I do if I lived? I'd stay in Japan . . . I want to live with these people. I want to die with these people."[47] There is a sympathy here that speaks directly to an imagined engagement between Japan and the West; a sympathy grounded in lived intimacy and shared civility, that provided for Keene an alternative to the language of bellicosity or of exploitation or of governance in the world. It is a sympathy utterly familiar to Hazzard in both its sensibilities and its diction: the seaming together of memory, loss, war, and poetry in a moment of supreme inwardness, and in literature's capacity for consolation. Keene's story in many important ways recalls Hazzard's own account of literary and linguistic self-fashioning in the provincial outer limits of the Anglophone mid-century, in Wellington, New Zealand, where, aged seventeen and suffering from a broken heart, she discovered the Italian Romantic poet Leopardi in translation and began to learn Italian in order to read the poems in the original. And just as Keene took up Japanese citizenship in 2012, after spending a half-century living between Manhattan, Capri, and Naples, Hazzard had herself been made an honorary citizen of Capri in 2000. Hazzard and Keene's twinned tales highlight literature's affinity with, and proximity to, translation and expatriation. For both, those moments of poetic identification are realized primarily in displacement.

The announcement of Keene's decision to apply for Japanese citizenship was received with enthusiasm and affection by the Japanese public: "Suddenly I was a hero." The formal politeness of his Tokyo neighbors changed: "Now, suddenly, I'm one of them. They say, 'Good morning,' and 'Take care of yourself.'"[48] He continued, in a later interview, "What I did, which was something minor and personal, became something of great importance . . . I became a famous person in a sense. And the Japanese were extremely grateful. I gave them what I could give them."[49] His adopted son, Seiki Keene said, "He devoted his life to Japanese Literature, and to become part of Japan's soil, as a Japanese person, was my father's longstanding dream."[50] For her part, Hazzard lived her last years far from both Australia and her adopted homes of Capri and Naples, prevented from returning to Italy by ill health. Keene's last letter, in 2008, to her carries all the poignancy of hindsight. He mentions the injury she had sustained the previous year, after which she lost mobility and slipped into dementia. Their friendship had been substantial for both. Their correspondence gives voice to that substance and offers to their readers a new and final view of their unforgettable lives.

1

1977–1986

NEW YORK, JANUARY 31, 1977

Dear Shirley

I am sure you could tell how much I enjoyed our conversation yesterday. The occasion that has brought us together was certainly a sad one, and many of the things we talked about were sad, but I am sure that in retrospect the afternoon will seem an unusually happy one because it was filled with the pleasure of making a new friend.

I am sending you the short piece I wrote about Ivan for <u>Monumenta Nipponica</u>, a journal published in Tokyo. I wrote two similar tributes for other places, but I haven't any copies of them.

Thank you again. I look forward to our next meeting.

Yours sincerely,
Donald

NEW YORK, AUGUST 17, 1978

Dear Donald—

I have tried several times to reach you by phone since coming back from Italy and finding your "Barren Years".[1] This work is immensely moving to us—as I'm sure to all its readers—and so important one somehow wishes to . . . what? to "distribute" it. One wishes, too, to speak with you. I thought you might not yet be in Japan, and scarcely know where to address this word of inadequate thanks and great admiration for this extraordinary document.

[. . .]

In July Ivan was two years dead—still quite hard to credit. I had a disagreeable phone conversation with Edita[2] in the winter (or spring, was it?), after you and I spoke on the phone. She declared she could not see me as I had "relations" with Annalita[3] (whom in fact I've seen twice since Ivan's death)—"corresponded" with her etc . . . I felt the injustice of this, but also the absurdity that someone should try to dictate who should be received in one's own house . . . Apparently, even the greatest griefs arouse enmities and egotisms, rather than large-mindedness. What an unhappy drama, and where will it ever end? What is its truth?

We work and are content—we return to Italy for Sept–Oct. If you should still be here, won't you call and come to see us? Otherwise it sounds a long time until January '79.

With thanks from the heart, and with high regard and much friendship—

Shirley

TOKYO, SEPTEMBER 6, 1978

Dear Shirley,

Thank you so much for your letter, which has been forwarded from New York. I shall be in Japan again until January. This has not only become my routine but is now a kind of necessity since the apartment I share in New York is on a six months' basis, so even if I returned before then I would have nowhere to go. When I made this decision I could not imagine I would ever wish to do otherwise, but I have begun to wonder now if I have not underestimated the importance to me of my life in New York.

I was extremely pleased by your (and Francis') kind words about "The Barren Years". These are literally the first reactions of any kind to the article, and I had managed to achieve some sort of oriental resignation about the fate of anyone who writes on subjects not of general interest. But to have as the first—and for all I care, the only—comments such praise has made me very happy. I sat down and reread the article on the spot. About fifteen years ago I wrote an article on a similar theme. It was much harsher. Curiously, it was a friend, the professor of Japanese at Moscow university, who said, "You must have been very young when you wrote it." I could imagine that she had had similar experiences. What I wrote then was not wrong, but I wanted to go beyond it, even to blot it out with something that showed greater compassion even though I am fundamentally very much opposed to militarism in any form. I rather expected people would be surprised, if only because (as far as I know) no one in the West and very few people in Japan have read the books in question for at least thirty years. But nothing—and then your wonderful comments. Thank you.

[. . .]

I'm sorry that you had the unpleasant telephone conversation with Edita, and I am afraid I am to blame. When I saw her & mentioned you to her she seemed eager to be in touch with you again. Heaven only knows how she found out that you had been in touch with Annalita.

[. . .]

My history of Japanese literature advances slowly. I find my interest in modern Japanese writers is shifting imperceptibly from their success as writers to what it meant as a Japanese to write in that way.

All my best wishes to you and Francis. I look forward very much to seeing you after my return.

Yours, Donald

NEW YORK, DECEMBER 21, 1979

A Happy Christmas, dear Donald, and all good things in 1980—we hope to see you here early in the New Year.

Since writing from Italy I've again read your Meeting with Japan[4]—one joy after another. [. . .]

Here we are well, at work, serene (malgrado lo stato del mondo) . . . A warm early December has given place to a frigid grey Christmas—certainly "two-overcoats" weather. For a new novel I need a famous, long or longish Chinese (preferably) or Japanese literary work as yet never translated. Can you provide one?

With love from us both—Shirley

USAMI, IZU PENINSULA, NOVEMBER 26, 1980

Dear Shirley and Francis,

My thoughts have been very much with you as more and more reports come in about the earthquake in southern Italy. Of course,

I know that you are not there, and that is a relief, but I'm sure you must have friends in the vicinity, and (though the reports in the Japanese press have not mentioned Capri) your house may also have been damaged. I hope that the tragedy, unspeakable as it is, has at least not directly affected you.

I am writing from my room in a building overlooking the sea. It is dusk and the mountains are dark against the bluish-grey sky. It is one of the loveliest places in Japan I know and I have bought a tiny apartment on the ninth floor of a building recently erected on one of the hills overlooking the bay. Today has been clearer than I have ever seen it here. The islands that are normally concealed by mist, sea-spray or whatever it may be, are clearly visible even now. But there is a terrible irony in all this: Japanese seismologists have predicted that the next major earthquake in Japan will be here.

I knew this, of course, when I bought the place, but a combination of oriental fatalism and occidental conviction that such things would never happen to me persuaded me to yield, against advice, to its temptations of having this view available whenever I wanted it. (Now that it is darker there are lights in pockets of the hills, and a train like an immense glow-worm is curling around the bay far below) but the news from Italy has made my gesture seem more foolish than even fatalistic.

My stay in Japan has been enjoyable on the whole, though I discovered that this was the year when, for totally different reasons, friends I had been accustomed to seeing every week became relatively inaccessible, putting me more on my own resources. I had a glorious week in Peking at the end of October that I will tell you about—if you wish, when I return to New York. I plan now to be back on January 18, and I'll get in touch with you as soon as the worst of the jet lag is over. I look forward very much indeed to seeing you again.

Last night there was a gathering in commemoration of Mishima's death,[5] exactly ten years ago. I was called on to "say a few words" and to my surprise and consternation I almost broke down, and could hardly keep speaking. What extraordinary things have happened to our friends!

Warmest wishes, Donald

NEW YORK, DECEMBER 26, 1980

My dear Donald—

Your letter took long to come, and arrived only just before your lovely card. I reply with some feeling—not exactly trepidation—of anxiety that I so much want to make known to you how your letter moved me, and may not be able to do that as I wish. First, your thought for our thoughts in the Italian tragedy, which in fact never leaves my imagination. And then your depiction of your own setting, which made your mountains present to me, also in the atmosphere that flows from a loved place. We have spoken about these things, and I remember your saying—writing—in your "Meeting with Japan" that you came to depend on Japan for your happiness and thus to be sure that Japan could console you also for unhappiness. There are many for whom such a place does not exist even in fancy, and part of my own conscious joy in merely being in "my" chosen land is the sense of luck that Flaubert describes on the Nile: of gratitude that one is able to realise all this and look on with that awareness. I think that you, like me, came to this after you were quite grown up, and having enjoyed other places meantime, though not with this particular calm exultation. In my case, the sense of place was scarcely existent in childhood, and was perhaps saved up for the intensified adult pleasure later on.

I have been thinking about going back to Naples and trying to "do something", perhaps to write an article to draw particular attention to some aspect and so on. We left just before the catastrophe happened. My first impulse was to go back. But Francis is so much against this and indeed I doubt I could be useful. So for the present the idea is in abeyance. Also, it's true that what I want most—and not just selfishly, or at least the selfishness is not in the simplest form—is to get on with my new work. So here I am, in the coldest days yet known to me in NY, going through the usual Christmas hurly-burly, etc. Of course there are many pleasant things—most of all seeing friends, and then expecting your arrival in three weeks or so (and I hope this letter will get to Japan before you leave). An English friend, Bruce Chatwin (wrote a book about being in Patagonia) was here briefly and particularly asked if we would arrange a meeting with you whom he greatly admires. He is returning to NY in February. He is a charmer and quite a fascinating person, more like a phenomenon that used to exist than a modern man. He is about forty, looks younger, was Sotheby's youngest director ever at about twenty-four, but bolted from that to "travel" in the old way, for adventures of the mind as well as eye and body and, as Custine said, "to visit other centuries." Well, will "get hold of him" when he returns (a baleful expression that, I always think). Tomorrow night we are going to Les Carmelites at the Metrop. Opera—a work that by no means meets Ivan's conditions for suitable opera, but an impressive one I think. Yes, what extraordinary things have happened to our friends, as you say. Ivan's death remains an unresolved event and—for that and other reasons—unabsorbed in the way that such sorrows usually are. Once in a while it comes over me quite freshly that we shall never meet again, and the same protest rises up at a mindless tragedy. There was an article here on the anniversary of Mishima's death—I kept it, and shall show it to you if you would be interested. Yes, emphatically, we would like to hear about your time in Peking. Having suffered from homesickness for the east since I left it over thirty years ago, I find it curious that I quite fear any return there. Yet I find I return to it increasingly in my writing.

About the world, the less said the better. We have been in touch by phone with our Neapolitan friends—all intact, but of course greatly distressed by the misery surrounding them. A poor man with large family, whom I have known since 1956, wrote me just now that they survived "con l'aiuto del Signore" the terrible experience, including the worst earthquake, which struck their house and "ci ha costretti, io e tutta la famiglia, a passare cinque notti di terrore e paura, all'addiaccio e in mezzo alla strada." Well, we have both—you and I, I mean—chosen the earthquake zone. Thank you for asking about Capri—there, they had only "fright", no damage. It would be a severe fright too, if one thinks of all those teetering crags that are the Caprese landscape.

The usual—or worse than usual—politics go on, and the inexorable false declarations by politicians. Do you remember, in "War and Peace", in the phase when Prince Andrei takes up a position on a govt committee and runs around seeing "important" people, how he notices in passing that he did the same thing more than once that day????

Let us meet soon—shall be in touch on your return. We must have a quiet evening here, and "laugh about things that are grave in the suburbs." Thank you again for your beautiful letter. With warmest new year greetings from us both, and with much affection from Shirley.

NEW YORK, SEPTEMBER 5, 81

Dear Donald—your welcome card comes just as I'm packing to return to Italy until mid-November. We've had some summer adventures, including a week at Tunis in June; but no plans for Australia or Japan at present, alas. However, I must send a quick word—ad interim—abt your own trip to Aust. Yesterday we had here at lunch a delightful friend, Edmund Capon, who is now director with the Gallery of NSW, at Sydney, and who longs to meet you. You no doubt know he is an orientalist, was with the V & A, is editor of "Oriental Art" (which, he says, you've contributed to); and he has already done much for Aust in, eg, organising a splendid travelling show of Chinese painting—some works which had never before left China. I am giving him yr Tokyo address—I hope that is alright?—and he will write to you. He is overjoyed to learn that you will be in Aust. [. . .]

My great friend at Sydney is a fine writer & lovely woman, Elizabeth Harrower; a great & gentle soul. She is in Mosman, NSW, 2088 (a seaside suburb of Sydney, where indeed I went to school—my ten years of defective but entire education . . .). [. . .] She knows masses of writers, painters, etc., but perhaps you will not want such jamborees and she is delightful to be alone with. [. . .] A quite different but also v nice woman is Mrs. Anne Lewis, a lively presence in the visual arts in Aust. [. . .] Then, Don Dunstan, former premier of the state of South Australia, who has a strong interest in oriental art and affairs, and arranged exhibitions of—eg Thai sculpture—Eastern art in Adelaide.

[. . .]

With love—Shirley

TOKYO, SEPTEMBER 19, 1981

Dear Shirley, thank you so much for your letter. It was good of you to write even while in the midst of packing. I shall treasure the information in your letter. I'm disappointed that you and Francis will not be there, but of course I realized how unlikely a coincidence that would have been.

My tour of New Zealand and Australia is being arranged by the Japan Foundation. They have decided that it is more effective to have a non-Japanese praise Japanese culture, rather than a Japanese who might be too diffident—or else a Japanese who would say, in the manner of a Sinhalese I once heard in New York, "Many, many years ago when your ancestors ran about in the forests of Europe with nothing but a smudge of blue to conceal their nakedness, my ancestors enjoyed a high degree of civilization."

The Japan Foundation people are extremely kind and helpful, but they also want to get their money's worth, so I will lecture at three places in New Zealand and five in Australia. Unfortunately, the only month I could get away for the necessary travel is December, precisely when the Australian universities are having their summer holidays. So I can't count on a ready-made audience. I will be lecturing in Australia in Melbourne, Canberra, Sydney, Brisbane and Perth. After reading your letter about Adelaide I decided I wanted to go there, but there just doesn't seem to be any possibility of adding another city, and the other five cities all have displayed special interest in Japanese studies.

[. . .]

My big news is that earlier this week I completed the manuscript of the two modern volumes of my history of Japanese literature.[6] Fourteen years! Of course, there will still be queries from the editor and various minor things to attend to, but it is a wonderful feeling. And I'm so glad that completion of the book will not be hanging over me when I go to Australia. It still hasn't really seeped into my brain that the book is done. I keep going into bookstores to look for this or that elusive volume I need, to realize that at some point I decided not to write about that particular author.

My book about opera singers also came out this week. It has a very youthful picture of Boris Christoff, among others. I doubt that any publisher would be interested in the English text of the book.

In Japan there is a curiously strong interest in writings by amateurs about the different arts, no doubt because the professionals tend to be so learned and so dreary as to dampen all pleasure in music or art criticism.

All my best to you and Francis.
Yours, Donald

POSTCARD, NAPLES, OCTOBER 22, 1981

Dear Donald—

Thank you so much for your letter; and our many many congratulations on completion of your mighty work. What labour, and what achievement. Francis says he has an inkling of what you feel. For me, the consummation of such an attempt is mind boggling. When we are all together again, we must celebrate it. Also—my Lord!—your book on opera singers. 1981 is annus mirabilis for you. (And here we have commemorations of the Bimillenario of the death of Virgil. This Tennysonian event v. moving in its manifestations . . .)

Don Dunstan was here briefly, & hopes very much to be in Sydney at the time of your visit. [. . .] Edmund Capon will have written you?—with love—Shirley.

BRISBANE, DECEMBER 15, 1981

Dear Shirley,

I'm now in what is undoubtedly the most luxurious hotel accommodation I have ever occupied. I have a bedroom of generous proportions, a sitting room for a considerable gathering, two bathrooms, a bar furnished with domestic & imported liquors, and clothes closets about the size of the hotel rooms I more normally occupy. The view of Brisbane from my windows on the 20th floor of the Lennox Plaza Hotel would be even better if it weren't raining, but I have successfully brought rain to every city in New Zealand and Australia I have visited, even some which were suffering from drought.

But what a delightful two weeks this has been! The first lecture, in Auckland, was attended by well over 500 people, the largest gathering by far, and the local paper reported formally on the professor from "Japan Columbia University". I liked Wellington which is built vertically along a thin strip of land between the mountains and the sea. Christchurch was quiet & rather English in appearance. Queenstown was remarkably beautiful.

But I needn't prolong the travelogue. My first purpose in writing was to tell you how kind your friends have been to me, & how much they have contributed to making this rather frantic tour of Australia into a memorable experience. [. . .]

Sydney was the only place where I had time to myself. [. . .] I was invited to dinner by the Capons, who had thoughtfully invited my friends plus the Japanese consul general & his wife. It was a thoroughly delightful evening, which might have lasted much longer if I had not had a lecture the next day.

I regret to say that I tried repeatedly without success to reach Elizabeth Harrower that day & rather despaired of ever finding her, but I finally got through & we arranged to have lunch together on Monday, the 14th. I can tell instantly why you and she are such great friends. We talked without reserve as if we had known each other for years. After lunch we walked here and there, still talking, went into a book shop where I bought some recent Australian novels & poetry. (I was also pleased to see an Australian paperback edition of The Transit of Venus.)

The talk in Sydney went well, I think. There was a large gathering, including a three-year-old girl in the second row who was on her best behavior and did not so much as yawn. [. . .] I went to a rather dull gathering at the House of the Japanese consul general, who (unlike the Capons) seems to have chosen his guests for their rank rather than their interest in the sorts of things that interest me. But that is uncharitable—it was a pleasant occasion that was simply not up to the exceptional occasions that have been provided by your friends.

This evening a lecture here in Brisbane, then tomorrow I leave for Perth. I'll have a few days to idle in the sun in Bali before returning to Japan. If it is cool & rainy in Brisbane where I know no one, I shall really be disappointed.

So thank you again for having made this so special a journey. My best wishes to you & Francis for Christmas and the New Year. I eagerly look forward to seeing you both in January.

Yours, Donald

NEW YORK, AUGUST 29, 1982

Dear Donald—

Thank you so much for your card—we tried to telephone you in NYC, thinking you might be here for those proofs you spoke of. As yet, no luck—"Nessun risposta"—so I send this word and enclosures to your Tokyo pad. If I were to cut out all the "Japanese" items in the NYT you'd be inundated. A burgeoning interest, thanks to you and a few other lofty souls.

The world is appalling—thank heaven people such as ourselves live, in part, "out" of it, in a longer "reality". One of Flaubert's best letters to Louise Colet tells of his young cook who knows nothing of the deposition of Bonaparte, restoration of the monarchy, etc etc.

Flaubert says: "That woman is a model for us all." While you've been suffering through floods, Italy (S from Florence, to Sicily) has had a horrific drought: <u>NO</u> rain for nearly six months, record-breaking & sustained heat. For the first time in all my memory, even Capri had days & nights never below 90° and often over 100°. The countryside is desolate—drought giving way to fires throughout the peninsula; except in the Lake district, where of course there is incessant rain. Meanwhile, NYC is <u>enjoying</u> August, a rational mixture of sunshine & clear nights . . .

[. . .]

Beautiful things we saw this summer. The world can be thrilling if left to its better self. Do you know the writings of Custine?—what a remarkable person, one splendid aphorism after another . . .

Your card is delightful. Rabbits seem to have lent themselves to anthropomorphism in a number of cultures. It must be that twitching visage that most suggests the human face . . .

[. . .]

—With much friendship from us both and with love—Shirley.

TOKYO, SEPTEMBER 24, 1982

Dear Shirley,

Thank you very much for your letter and for the various articles you enclosed. Thank you and Francis also for having written the man at the New York Times about Ivan. The article was welcome, but it was written on the basis of what an informant at Princeton told him—or so it seems anyway. Ivan was never given due recognition by the professional Japanologists. I am not sure why this was so. He did not write learned articles for obscure orientalist periodicals, it is true, but his extraordinary translations of The Pillow Book or the diary which he called As I Crossed A Bridge of Dreams were ample proof of his ability to handle gracefully even rather difficult materials. He made mistakes, some of them rather elementary, because he really had not lived long enough in Japan to acquire the everyday knowledge that one cannot easily acquire from books. Because he spent relatively little time in Japan he was also unknown to the Japanese public. That may be why he never received a decoration or similar recognition from the Japanese government. After his death I addressed several pleas to the officials concerned that he be given a posthumous decoration; but obviously he had enemies or at any rate people who were unwilling to give him what he so clearly merited. I am glad that you wrote the letter. It is unlikely that they will do a supplementary article in the near future, but they presumably will keep the letter on file for whenever the time comes for another article on Japanese literature.

The copy-edited text of my manuscript has been reaching me with the agonising slowness. The complete manuscript was delivered last October. The publishers did nothing about it until February, when it was sent to an aged and infirm copy editor. She disgorged one chunk in June and another in August, and I have been waiting for the third and final section ever since. It takes me approximately four days to do what she takes four or five months to do. Her main concern seems to be to make this the first absolutely non-sexist history of Japanese literature. Mankind is always replaced by humankind, and if I refer to the reader as "he", this is naturally changed to "he or she". And the word "person" is used so often it becomes ludicrous. "If a person meets a person and that person . . ." I have restored my original versions only occasionally. It is not a matter for which I am prepared to die. But I know, though the copy editor does not, that in Japanese everyone, man and woman, single and married, is referred to as—san, and there is no trace of equality between the sexes.

I don't know when if ever I will receive proofs. The editor-in-chief at Holt has moved to Simon & Shuster. He was directly responsible for my book. I hope that the change will not affect the production schedule. It could hardly make it any slower. At the moment I have no plans for returning to New York, so I am trying to get invited to a conference about a year from now. I hate conferences, but they seem to provide pretexts for going almost anywhere. Somehow I do not think that scholarship is so unlike writing of other kinds; it is best done by oneself.

I have had some pleasant exchanges of letters with Bill Weaver, who very kindly sent me a fine book of essays by himself and others on Verdi. I have also had a letter from Elizabeth Harrower which I have been slow to answer. I do hope that you are able to invite her to New York. In the same way that I found my trip to Australia stimulating I think that she would enjoy New York, especially with you to introduce her to interesting people.

I can't remember whether or not I told you, but I have become a "guest editor" of the Asahi Shimbun, the leading Japanese newspaper.[7] It was most unexpected, and I still do not really know what they hoped for from me, but I have been moved by the honor. There is a danger of diverting my energies in so many directions that I lose sight of my main task, finishing my history of Japanese literature, but it is hard to decline when offered that kind of honor.

I hope that the weather is better in Italy. The rain you have missed is all here. It has rained every single day of September. We are up to typhoon #19 and, to tell the truth, I'm rather bored with typhoons now. If only I could think of some way of sending you one . . .

All my best to you and Francis.
Yours, Donald

CAPRI, OCTOBER 28, 1982

Dear Donald—

Many many thanks for your most welcome letter. [. . .] The account of your experiences with copy editing was just about unbearable to both of us. That humourless form of feminism, embodied in the "chairperson" mentality, in particular drives me bonkers. It is another bureaucratic tyranny forced on us in the name of tolerance and equity—ie in the name of reasonableness, one is supposed to accept un-reason. The rest of your sufferings make the head spin. It is inconceivable that an unqualified person should presume to alter meanings in a work of scholarship of this kind and quality. [. . .]

How well you put it, that scholarship is not so unlike writing of other kinds. Indeed—but when it is done well, as with writing of other kinds also. Something appalling has happened with scholarship in America—not only the extremes of the literary shambles in academe, but for instance art history, the "social sciences" etc. Thank God we still know many exemplary scholars and devoted teachers; but they are often embattled within the scholarly context. A legendary figure here at Naples, the historian Roberto Pane—a man now probably over eighty, impassioned, quarrelsome, fearless, imperious, vain, immensely knowledgeable, witty, polymathic, tireless . . . —was inveighing the other day to us against some immense work on Bernini produced by a Princeton prof called Levin (I think), which apparently reproduces every last detail of every minute evidence of Bernini's life without distinction, etc. Pane, leaping from his chair with outrage, burst out against this author's insensibility towards historical experience: "He mentions the Counter-Reformation in passing—in passing!—as if it were no more than a road accident. To us—who have it still (drawing fingers down his arm) on our very skin!" ("La Contriforma!—che noi abbiamo sempre sulla pelle!")

Bravo for the guest editorship of the Asahi Shimbun. Something unimaginable to me, this degree of mastery of another language and such a difficult one, such a complex series of nuances. The same Roberto Pane mentioned above is editor of "Napoli Nobilissima"— a deservedly revered series of monographs published by scholars on matters touching the history of Naples; from time to time (every twenty years or so) these are bound into volumes. This has been going on for about a century. He has asked me to contribute: an honour undeserved and never hoped. I have an (unlearned) idea, on certain experiences of poets at Naples (not the well-covered ground of Goethe, etc). But even for a brief article of few pages, am daunted by the quality of written Italian required. Apart from the possibility of a mistake in grammar or in subtlety of usage, there is a question of tone and originality of language that determines me. Anyway I can't do it at present. When I get to it, shall write it in English, translate it, and see how I feel. These matters of course don't bother me when I'm writing letters or some casual document in Italian—but a literary work shld have style . . .

A propos—I have reread all the Kawabata novels I can find in translation, these past weeks and months. What a master. All the novels I have are translated by Seidensticker except one ("Beauty and Sadness", trans. by Hibbett). I find the translation—rather, the English—often disturbing; even vulgar. Can see it must be immensely difficult. The trouble is with the translator's lack of refinement in his own tongue. I wonder what you think. "The Master of Go" is the best of the translations; how appallingly hard that must have been to translate. As far as I can tell—and forgive such an ignorant judgement—it seems Kawabata's masterpiece. A wonderful book, enviable. I would have loved to have written it.

Yes, we do hope 1983 will bring Elizabeth to New York. What a good idea, that it might bring forth her writing gift. I'm going to tell her that you proposed that. She exists as something luminous in my mind; some suggestion of a great soul in my consciousness.

Such beauty here—never ending. Last week we spent a day at Ninfa, south of Rome. An incredible place, a dream. Shall tell you when we meet. As to "being bored with typhoons"—after a burning, rainless summer, we had an onslaught of equinoctial tempests; and I thought of your typhoon observation. However, many glorious days, including today . . . With much affection—Shirley

[. . .] PS: Thank you for your words about Ivan. We will talk more of this, perhaps. For me, he is an exemplary instance of Empson's line, "all losses haunt us"—meaning, or unresolved events. I never really believe in his death.

NEW YORK, NOVEMBER 7, 1982

Dear Donald—

[. . .] The day after my return we did an adventurous thing for New Yorker stick in the muds—hired a car and went to the Botanic Garden at the Bronx to see a beautiful display of chrysanthemums in the conservatory there, prepared for the past eighteen months by a Japanese chrysanthemum expert—I feel the inadequacy of that designation, but know no western term for this poetic vocation. Of course these flowers ceased to be chrysanthemums in our sense. Odd for me—having just come from the Italian Day of the Dead: Tutti Santi is a tremendous day in Italy, and remains a focus on ancestor worship in a manner often moving and beautiful. Millions of chrysanthemums are taken to cemeteries throughout Italy, people often travelling long distances to visit graves. (Profanely I may add that it is a fine opportunity to get into churches often closed at other times, and to see pictures one otherwise has to get special permission for. In Rome last Monday—the day of the holiday—I profited somewhat from that, and in the course of it heard at least one quite delightful sermon. A day of splendid warm weather, at noon the entire populace of Rome appeared in the streets well dressed from church and a sort of decorous festival took place—rather like Easter Sunday—with large family lunches in restaurants outdoors etc. Even allowing for advantages of climate and temperament, a marked contrast with, say, an English public holiday in a large city . . .)

However, I intended to say that a present of a bunch or plant of chrysanthemums in Italy is <u>not</u> well regarded: tantamount to saying, Drop Dead. The flower has that rather sacred function of remembering the dead, and can't be thought of as cheering up a living-room.

[. . .]

Please, when you have a moment, let us know about yr expected return to NYC . . . With much affection from us both—Shirley.

TOKYO, DECEMBER 7, 1982

Dear Shirley,

Having just typed the date, my mind flies back to December 7, 1941. I had just gone with the Japanese friend to Staten Island, and when we returned on the ferry boat to the Battery, a newsboy was hawking the New York Inquirer with the headline "JAPS ATTACK PEARL HARBOR".

I remember that day very clearly, even to the faces of some of the people in the subway. But I am hard put to explain why I have not written you during the past month. I have been busy, of course, but I never take that as an excuse for not writing. I have certainly thought of you and Francis often enough, but I suppose that I have not written chiefly because I have been reluctant to reveal the awful truth that I may not return to New York at all in 1983. Normally I would be returning in January, but this will be my 13th year teaching without sabbatical leave (as opposed to unpaid leave). Unlike full-time teachers, who get a sabbatical leave every seventh year, I get mine in the thirteenth year. When I made the decision to stay in Japan for the entire time I thought with delight of seeing the spring in Japan for the first time in almost twenty years. (I did not go to Japan in the spring when I had my last sabbatical leave.) I thought with even greater pleasure of the immense amount of work I would be able to accomplish during the unbroken period of eighteen months. I did not sufficiently think of how much I would miss my friends in New York. Nor, alas, did I anticipate the number of distractions that have effectively kept me from doing my work. That is the unhappy truth that has kept me from writing you. Of course, it would not be impossible to fly back to New York. There are cheap plane tickets on airlines you have not heard of, by circuitous routes over the South Pole or possibly the Gobi Desert. But I have irrevocably let my apartment in New York for the spring, and it would be strange and perhaps unpleasant to be in New York and unable to get my own books or rummage through bottom drawers for papers I stuffed away when I left.

[. . .]

I enjoyed your account of Roberto Pane leaping from his chair in indignation over the book on Bernini that failed to treat the Counter-Reformation. Somehow I recalled a poetry reading given by Giuseppe Ungaretti in New York (at Columbia). I had met him the day before at a party, and found him so extraordinary that, although my Italian is really restricted to what people say in Verdi operas, I persuaded myself that I would understand him. I might have, but he began the lecture with a burst of uncontrolled rage because, on visiting the Museum of Modern Art that day, he had discovered that there were no paintings on display by an artist (I unfortunately forget who it was) whom he admired. I was struggling desperately to follow what was being said, but all I was really aware of was that something unspeakable had happened. Almost as bad as not giving the Counter-Reformation its due!

I am glad that you liked Kawabata's novels. <u>The Master of Go</u> was Ivan's favorite, and probably was Kawabata's own. Unlike Ivan, however, I'm unable to figure out the simplest puzzle, ever, and I could neither follow nor ignore the moves in <u>Go</u>. I shall re read it, after what you have said.

[. . .] All my best to you and Francis for Christmas. As ever, Donald

NEW YORK, JANUARY 19, 1983

Dear Donald—

[. . .]

My own recollection of "JAPS ATTACK PEARL HARBOR" was riding on the top of a bus, home from school outing with my "best friend", a pigtailed blonde who now has grandchildren, and seeing the poster "PEARL HARBOUR, MANILA, DARWIN BOMBED". I wonder if this is accurate—whether they were all bombed in the same day—or if I have telescoped a couple of days together in my mind. But that is what I recall. It was a blazing hot day, & the "feeling" of the day is very strong to me. I was nine. I was a generation older when another moment arrived, in 1945, a winter morning when I was dressing to go to school and heard on "the wireless" that the atomic bomb had been dropped. Many episodes from the war are very clear to me, in their atmosphere as well as the facts. I remember for instance picking up the afternoon newspaper in our driveway and reading that the German armies were "ten miles from Moscow". And, earlier, "HITLER'S DEPUTY FLIES TO SCOTLAND." All the time of the blitz is v clear to me. Then,

Australia was having constant adventures, unlike its old self: Japanese submarines blown up one night in Sydney Harbour, Americans in uniform by the tens of thousands; tremendous wartime shipping—which we were forbidden to mention, although we could sail around and around all the ships and wave to the unmentionable sailors . . . Near the end of the war, the delirious welcome to the British fleet, Mountbatten's excursions over aircraft carriers, battleships. The Queen Mary and the Queen Elizabeth, unmentionable too, had been in the harbour—they had been unattainable legends until then. Soldiers in battle dress from the jungle (Australian battle dress made a wretched showing beside the Americans . . .), with dark yellow or green faces from "atabrine". What times we have passed through and somehow survived.

I wonder what happened to your Japanese friend after his return with you from Staten Island.

I shld confess right away that I could not possibly follow the game of Go in the novel. But I didn't find it necessary. This no doubt would rightly be scorned by those who care deeply that the full meaning of the novel should be present; but since I thought the book marvellous in any case, I don't feel too badly. I urged it on Francis, who read it at once and, when he put it down, said, "A masterpiece." I too shirk puzzles, although I proudly claim skill with the London Times crossword, the only crossword I ever do. It is witty and literary, and only occasionally unfairly obscure I think. However, at first untutored glance I think it must seem insane.

I met Ungaretti when he was at Columbia. It was at dinner at the Breunigs. I had a delightful time with him, but felt I could not establish any real rapport in so short a time, or in the way I would have liked . . . I wonder who the painter was whose exclusion from MOMA so infuriated him?—Morandi? De Chirico? De Pisis? Guttuso? . . . It wld be interesting to know. At present in NY we have the Vatican treasures (well, a small portion of them) about to break on us. Many delightful things have presented themselves this winter—we went to a supreme Lucia di L, Sutherland and Alfredo Kraus. One of the most beautiful evenings I've ever spent. Last night we went to the ballet (the formless "Don Quixote"), first night; Nureyev was stupendous—even the NY Times admits it this morning. One sees that he is older, yet the incredible feats and the magic take place. Afterwards we were asked to a party for him at Sardi's (not our usual existence I assure you), and had a good time: it is nice to see the young dancers, still beautiful off stage. Many other things done, also some work. F's Vol II of Flaubert's letters has had a fine reception—he is glad to have the new printings as he catches many graves turned into acutes etc.

[. . .]

I wonder if you ever read Montale? His poetry is difficult, but there are some moderately good translations. However, the essays— recently translated in a large selection and published here—are full of highly intelligent and thoughtful observations. He is one of the few people who seem to write dispassionately and with strong opinions on the "dehumanization of art", which becomes a preoccupation to me. I wonder if art will go on in any recognizable form, and if so will there be anything other than "mass art". I scarcely believe there will; but one hopes to be disappointed in such pessimism. In an interview, Montale remarked—of all the rationalizers of why contemporary art necessarily takes its current forms—"I do not deny that they must follow such paths; I only deny their right to call themselves free men."

Like many cultivated Italians, he often—though not always—got off the track when he commented on foreign life & art, and especially when he incorporated such comments into his poems. Someone (a lesser figure by far, at least to me) who gets hopelessly bushed when he sets foot abroad is John Updike: his writings set in Italy for instance set one's teeth on edge. Thus I wonder what you may have thought of his article in last week's (3 Jan) New Yorker on Tanizaki and Soseki? It may be that Updike is better in Japan than elsewhere, but his "European" writings cause me to doubt . . . A propos, Mr. Stephen Shaw from Kodansha International sent me a translated novel I've not yet had time to read: "Child of Fortune" by Yuko Tsushima. When I suggested he should send one also to Updike, he forwarded me another copy, and I've sent it on accordingly. I wonder if you know this writer, and what you think of the book if so?

All publishers pronounce this "a bad time" to publish. Yet, in twenty years of producing books, I've yet to hear from a publisher that it was "a good time" to publish. There has always been a dire reason why one was publishing at just the wrong time. Yet books have gone on and lived a life of their own.

[. . .]

"Things" in the world of course seem as if they could scarcely be worse, and no doubt that is in many places true. However, I remember one brilliant Sunday morning in London when we were walking through Belgravia to visit—I think—my mother in a nearby hotel— about a dozen years ago—and we took conscious note of the fact that this was all possible: beauty, civility, some relative degree of liberty, decency, justice, absence of fear. And that historically it had come about against the odds. To manifest themselves against the odds is perhaps in the nature of civilised things; although the groundswell producing them is long and arduous, they have a freakish existence too, an element of almost constant surprise.

[. . .] In mid-March we are off to Italy for just a month. At San Carlo at Naples, there is a production of Mussorgsky's "Salambô"; and we also take a little trip down to Reggio Calabria to see "the bronzes of Riace", those colossal Greek 5th c. BC statues found in the sea a few years ago, now restored and on view to an astounded public (which we hope will not have arrived in late March; although by Easter the crowds will presumably re-emerge). All thrilling.

Much affection, and we do hope to see you sometime during 1983. [. . .] We wonder when your publication date is? I wish I knew the appropriate Japanese expression for trois fois merde, or Auguri—as ever—Shirley

NEW YORK, JANUARY 20, 1983

Dear Shirley,

[. . .]

Today I emerged unscathed from what the Japanese call <u>nin-gen dokku</u>, which means literally a "human dock". This neologism refers to the practice of having a complete medical examination that requires one to spend at least two days in the hospital while every conceivable test is performed, and it owes its peculiar name to the analogy between the services performed at the hospital and the rather similar services performed on a ship in dry dock. This is not a bad example of how the Japanese have expanded our poor old English language in a manner that would surprise Dr Johnson. Anyway, the worst feature of my present physical condition is a tendency to stooped shoulders, an occupational hazard with writers, I am told. I was particularly pleased that there are no conspicuous signs of old age creeping over me. There is still much work for me to do—or at least I think so.

I had a three week vacation in India and Thailand, returning to Japan on the 10th of this month. I enjoyed the sunshine and the heat. Unlike my previous visits to that part of the world, I was not bothered by the oppressive humidity. In fact, I was there during the one month or possibly six weeks of the year when the weather is hot but comfortable. In Bangkok I met a friend who was in New York last year, and to my surprise I received the enclosed photographs of Francis, taken at the annual festivities of the American Academy. Somehow, if one put that scene into a novel, no one would believe it: I just happened to meet someone in Bangkok who just happened to be carrying around some colored photographs of Francis Steegmuller.

Shortly after my return to Tokyo I had a telephone call from Kazuo Nakajima, the friend of Bill Weaver. He was to return to Italy in a couple of days, but we arranged a meeting and spent a most agreeable two or three hours in conversation. Just imagine teaching Japanese in Venice! Why didn't I think of that? I have visited Venice several times, briefly each time, but it just becomes more and more beautiful in my memory. It occurs to me that this is just the opposite of Proust's experience; his Venice was above all the Venice he could not visit, and the impossibility of going there made it seem so incomparably beautiful. But my Venice is one above all of silence, broken only by the occasional vaporetto, a city of human beings rather than of means of transportation.

Speaking of Proust, I have slowly been making my way through the new translation by Terrence Kilmartin. I find it quite wonderful, much better than my recollections of Scott Moncrieff, and really not very different from my recollections of reading the original. But, naturally, even more than the ease and grace of the translation it is the book itself that overwhelms me. Each page brings a new discovery—and I thought I knew Proust well.

On the plane going to India, believe it or not, I read Villette, which you once recommended. I thought that with the exception of one chapter which baffled me, the book was remarkably good, perhaps the most effective portrayal of desperate loneliness that I have ever read. The one chapter is towards the end, a dreamlike sequence in which Lucy creeps out of the house at night and makes her way to the center of the city where she sees almost everyone she knows, overhears their conversations, is even waved to from a carriage. It reads exactly like delirium, but the next chapter makes it clear that everything actually happened as described. And the mystery of the ghostly nun seems curiously unworthy of the book. Having said what no doubt many others have also said, I must add that I am most grateful to you for having called my attention to a book that moved me more than any novel of that period. It baffles me now why no one before you ever mentioned it to me.

[. . .]

All good wishes for what is still a relatively new year!
Yours, Donald

NEW YORK, JANUARY 25, 1983

Dear Donald—

A postscript to my letter of last week, in response to your delightful one just received. I'm taking it over to the hospital in a little while so that Francis can enjoy it and also for the pleasure of seeing his face (in the flesh) when <u>he</u> sees his face (in the photographs). As I've said, in a novel, one would never dare put the real coincidences of life into a novel. He—Francis—is fine, and in a few days can come home and, as the doctors say, forget all about his recent adventures. He will be glad to learn the expression <u>ningen dokku</u>, and still more glad to hear that your only defect is stooped shoulders. We had not even noticed this let alone imagined any other.

Yes, how fine to have been in India and SE Asia in these weeks. I remember, in my first autumn in Hong Kong, how suddenly one day I realised it was cool, it was dry or at least drier. The era before air conditioning too. Having met Kazuo any number of times, I learn only from you that his name is Nakajima—yes, he is a genius to be teaching Japanese in Venice. Your words about Venice, most <u>a proposito</u>, as—having shirked the tremendous expense of Venice hotels, even fairly ordinary ones, for some years—we are promising ourselves at least a week there soon. I'm interested in yr observations about the new Proust. First, for me, it is the fact that it has important passages not hitherto available in translation. But I don't agree with Richard Howard's review in the New York Times savaging Scott Moncrieff in favour of this new one. For one thing, the new translators clearly state that they have based their work on SM's. Then—I spent some weeks with my evening game of setting out the three and comparing; and for my own taste SM still sometimes wins out—although indeed I found passages in the new translation also at times simplified and improved. However, look at this (from my "favourite" passage, Albertine's letter of farewell): The French—from memory, I think correct—is "Croyez que, de mon côté, je n'oublierai jamais cette promenade deux fois crépusculaire, parce que la nuit venait et nous allions nous quitter," which Scott Moncrieff translates: (again from my memory) "Please believe that I shall never forget that drive in a twilight that was twofold because night was coming and we were about to part," and (new translation—from the book): "You may be sure that for my part I shall never forget that doubly crepuscular drive (since night was falling and we were about to part) and that it will be effaced from my memory etc." "Doubly crepuscular"? Brackets? Perhaps it is really, as Guizot said of Gibbon, that once someone has hewn out so great a work (in this case of translation) it is then possible to make objections to it since it now exists to object to, whereas was previously unimaginable, a labour one cld scarcely conceive.

So glad you like Villette—nice to think of it being read by you in Japan. We'll talk of it when we meet again. Please don't come when we are in Italy if you make your New York trip in the spring, as we greatly hope you will. We'll be in NYC again from mid-April to mid-May (then from late July to Labour Day). After this exceptionally mild winter we have a few cold days now, but already some thoughts of spring come to the imagination and 5:00 o'clock is no longer nightfall (although "doubly crepuscular") . . .

How good that your work is going on. I'm trying to remain on my own during this absence of F's in hospital, and get a good stretch of difficult stuff completed. As soon as one can get to it, a tremendous relief descends, don't you find?

Thank you so much for your coals-of-fire letter. All affectionate greetings from us both—yours—Shirley.

TOKYO, MARCH 28, 1983

Dear Shirley,

[. . .]

I'm spending my time in Japan quite happily. Progress on my book, the last of the four volumes of my history of Japanese literature, have been delayed pleasantly by the arrival of the first batch of galleys. I now believe that they will actually publish the book, though it has been almost two years since I turned over the manuscript. Galleys are in good condition, but at some point, after I last saw the manuscript, a kind and helpful editor made her way through the foot notes hacking them to pieces. Although she knows no Japanese, she has been instinctively aware, she thinks, of which words in a Japanese title are important, and she has deleted the rest. Or she has cut off the second half of a title, deciding it was too long, but because she has no idea of what the title means, they tend to end up in the form of <u>The Transit Of</u>. She shortened the title of my book <u>Modern Japanese Literature</u> to <u>Japanese Literature</u>, saving six letters; however this might prove confusing to some readers since I have another, quite distinct book called <u>Japanese Literature</u>. [. . .]

You asked in a previous letter if I had read Montale. Unfortunately I haven't. My Italian is entirely self-taught, mainly from opera libretti, and although I can read newspapers and the like, my knowledge of Italian is inadequate for poetry.

[. . .]

As ever, Donald

TOKYO, AUGUST 24, 1983

Dear Shirley,

I know what a long time it has been since I last wrote, and I apologize. The thought of writing you has been much in my mind, if only because I would like to have a letter in return, but my time has been divided up into such peculiar segments that there never seemed to be the right moment for resuming our correspondence.

[. . .]

My chief occupation has been writing a newspaper serial. This sounds rather like Dickens, but my serial has been devoted not to a novel, but to a study of Japanese diaries over the centuries. It is extremely difficult for me to write a manuscript of an absolutely prescribed length, and this means that I generally have to go over each instalment with an editor in order to fit it into the Procrustean space allotted to me. It has taken up far more time than I expected, but the time has not been wasted because I will be able to use my new knowledge when writing the first (concluding) volume of my history of Japanese literature. The greatest pleasure, predictably, has been discovering diaries I had never previously read. One, for example, was written by a woman in her eighties, and consists almost entirely of expressions of bitterness over the decision of her son, an eminent Buddhist priest in his sixties, to go to China in order to study at the fountainhead of his particular sect of Buddhism. She writes as if she has been completely deserted, though another son, also a Buddhist priest, is nearby. She curses her son and finally even Buddha for allowing so terrible, so unprecedented a calamity to happen to her. Then she curses herself for having lived so long. If only she had died earlier—she was sickly as a child—she would have been spared this anguish. The son, who seems like a monster, was probably a very pious man who was sure that he would see his mother in paradise, provided he did everything while in this world to ensure salvation for both of them. It is an amazing document (twelfth century), but it also made me realize for the first time, at least in words, how extremely important the relationship is between mothers and sons in Japan, and how extremely unimportant, certainly when compared to the west, the relationship is between fathers and daughters. Some Japanese soldiers died in 1945 with the cry "Long live the emperor!" on the lips, but many, many more died with the cry of "Mother!" or some diminutive instead. This made me realize, by a leap of association, how few operatic duets there are for mother and son as opposed to father and daughter. The only one I can think of is Azucena and Manrico in <u>Trovatore</u>, and they are really not even related. But how many Verdi operas are built around the father-daughter relationship. I haven't thought of any explanation for this difference between Japan and the West, and perhaps there isn't any, but this is the kind of reward I receive for battling my way through some almost forgotten diary.

The other day the enclosed review appeared in the Asahi evening news. I thought it might interest you, because I know your views are quite different. The reviewer, James Kirkup, has lived in Japan for many years, teaching English. I met him once, about 25 years ago. Very briefly, but I have had indirect contacts with him from time to time. He can be very nasty in his reviews, and he is in fact a kind of menace because of his conviction that he is the only person who can translate Japanese poetry. (I don't think he knows any Japanese, but he works with translations made by students.)

I hope that you and Francis have been well and enjoying Italy. I am looking forward very much to my return to New York in January. I really miss my friends in New York.

As ever,
Donald

NEW YORK, SEPTEMBER 10, 1983

Dear Donald—

Your letter was received with so much pleasure. I too have been intending as ever to write—do you think if we didn't "write" in our professional lives we'd take up the private pen more often? I think I said to you before this that I feel I am drowning in unanswered letters that—although pleasant to receive—mean little to me; while the friends I truly would like to write to go to the wall. Francis and I between us certainly write a thousand letters or more a year, nearly all of necessity. Elizabeth H and I have the expression "sending telexes" (or teleces . . .) for the messages we write in our heads to each other, which comparatively seldom get onto letter paper.

[. . .]

Next Thursday I leave for Italy. Francis follows ten days later. I should have been on Capri two weeks ago. But this year we had a misadventure as we were leaving Naples to come here for our August stay. When I tell you that for a lifetime we have told all our visitors to Naples that nothing can happen to them if only they will not carry anything snatchable, you will wonder why we had a bag in hand on our last evening in the city in late July. (In fact, we had been delivering books to a binder; and were being careful, staying near the wall etc.)

However, when we crossed an open space to a taxi, to return home, two youths on a Vespa who must have been stalking us flashed past, grabbed the bag; Francis held onto it for a second—enough to get flung to the ground and dragged. Terrible moments. (The drama quickly improves, I should say at once.) Street people were indescribably good. Police came. Two (quite other) young men told me not to wait for the ambulance but to put F in their car, and thus we sped to a nearby hospital. Disintegrating premises, excellent & efficient, humane care. X rays, etc. I phoned to a Neapolitan friend who, before I could finish speaking, said "I'm coming at once" and hung up. Stayed with us throughout the night—at a second hospital where we were sent to a specialist in head injuries. (It was Saturday night in July, and this specialist was at his country place on the sea. When called he too started at once; took an hour and a half to arrive; came at midnight, spent two hours with Francis.) Pronounced the injuries as restricted to a broken nose & contusions, possibly a cracked cheekbone. The other serious injury was a broken—right—shoulder. The contusions, blood, etc made everything look more appalling, of course. Upshot of all was that we made our plane to NY two days later, with superhuman help & comfort from friends, the airline, the doctors etc. (The Naples hospitals would not accept a penny from us—for X rays, ambulance, hours of doctors.) Once restored to the medical Mecca of NYC, all hell broke loose. I suppose this is a good place if you have—god forbid—a complex complaint; and a lot of money. But the neglect of a broken shoulder and nose was formidable, and resulted in terrifying haemorrhages from the nose, and a dawn admission to NY Hospital ten days after our return. A week in hospt fixed most things, except for patience with the shoulder which is now restored except for continuing exercises for mobility etc. F lost weight—it has been mercilessly and infernally hot. He also had a week of depression, presumably a delayed reaction—throughout the episode itself he was completely composed and even humorous.

So—long story, which explains our presence in NYC at this moment. F sees the shoulder doctor last time before joining me later this month; then we hope to remain in Italy until about 12 Nov. To think that when we return here you will be within a few weeks of your own re-entry. I confess I find the city awful in a variety of ways. However, there are great compensations—of friends, liveliness, music, pictures, and other assets (yesterday, a Metrop Museum friend let us in, in advance, to the Manet exhibition; a strangely variable painter in quality, to my mind, but of course with many astonishing talents). Since your departure, an appalling edifice has opened at 57th and Fifth, the Trump Tower, a temple to crass materialism. It carries with it an implication of—Dallas, perhaps; or some brash, indistinct but organised arrangement for flaunting wealth. Trumpery Tower. [. . .]

I was baffled—completely—by James Kirkup's view of P. White's autobiography. It is inconceivable to me that such an impression can be gained from a work of so much vindictiveness, such untransmuted egotism and revenge. Of course there are good things in it—the pieces about Greece, episodes in the war, in England, in the Middle East; youth in the Australian countryside. But wherever a direct personal comment enters, there is the danger—usually consummated—of an attack on something or someone. At one stage he says that Manoly (his long companion) says "I even hate him too". If not, Manoly seems the lucky exception. The attack on the painter Sidney Nolan, PW's greatest nonsexual friend for thirty years, is pretty insane. (Derives from Nolan's having remarried after his wife Cynthia's death—she was a suicide.) PW says "What I cannot forgive is his laying his head on another woman's breast"—Does not this strike you as unhinged? Who is he to "forgive", what is there to forgive, why proclaim this to the world? This is the man who gives, as his "recreation" in Who's Who: "Friendship" . . .

Disheartening, this also.

Time to go to Italy.

Your "serial" sounds utterly fascinating. I find it surprising that, at such an era, a Japanese woman would feel herself in a strong enough position to resent a son's defection (even if in the cause of Buddhism). I must think about opera. It is strange that more examples of Mother-Son do not come to mind, as one cannot stay in Italy even a matter of days without discovering how immensely important the mother-son relation is. Now of course subject to some erosion; but, for an older generation, sacred. "La Mamma" is not only the Madonna and Cybele, but a natural force, something that throbs through Italian life. Yes, of course, Trovatore, and the dread line: "Ero già figlio prima d'amarti". Turiddu and Mama Lucia. Well, we have to work on this.

[. . .]

Much to ask, much to exchange. We look forward to all that. Meantime—[. . .] warmest friendship and affection from us both— Shirley.

TOKYO, DECEMBER 17, 1983

Dear Shirley,

I feel thoroughly ashamed of myself for not having answered your fine letter, but I have already received my punishment by not having been favored by another letter since then. How to explain my silence, given the fact that I enjoy writing letters and am normally a good correspondent? I suppose it is because I have felt that when writing to you I had to maintain a certain standard of literacy which is not expected by most other correspondents. So I put off writing until I had time to think, my mind was fresh, etc. The problem is that I have really been very busy, and the choice has always been between sending a poor letter and no letter at all, and I am afraid that I have chosen the latter. Today I shall choose the former!

My busyness has come from an unexpected quarter. In July I was asked by the Asahi Shimbun to write a serial on Japanese diaries. I have been very much interested in Japanese diaries ever since my wartime experiences. For about a year I did nothing but read diaries taken from the bodies of Japanese soldiers killed in various parts of the Pacific area. I developed a skill at reading difficult or just plain bad handwriting that is still useful, but I also first became aware of Japanese as people in a specially intimate sense. One might say that the first Japanese people I ever knew well were all dead before I made their acquaintance through their diaries. Most diaries began (before the soldier or sailor left Japan) with stereotyped expressions of fervent patriotism. I later learned that diaries were regularly inspected by petty officers to make sure that the writers held the approved sentiments. But once the writer was alone or in a small unit surrounded by the enemy, he dropped all pretenses and expressed exactly what he actually felt. Or, at any rate, this happened often enough to make reading the diaries an intermittently absorbing experience.

So, when I accepted this assignment of writing five episodes a week on Japanese diaries I did it without much apprehension of possible difficulties. But as I started to write I realized that I could only do this kind of work with my entire energies. It could not be something I dashed off, though a light conversational series would probably have been more to the taste of the public than what I have actually been writing. I started with the first literary diaries, from the ninth century, and I have steadily ploughed my way through most of the literary diaries until 1600. This has meant reading many minor works whose existence I never suspected. I have always been able to find <u>something</u>, no matter how unpromising the diary at first seemed to be. I have now written 131 episodes. [. . .]

It has been something of an education, but it has taken me away from what should be my main task, completing my history of Japanese literature. Work on the first volume (the early history) stopped in its tracks in July, and although I can use some of the diary material, I have really been prodigal with a limited amount of time at my disposal.

The two modern volumes of the history are scheduled to appear in April. The original publication date was May 1983, but the size of the books seems to have stunned everyone. The two books will amount to some 2000 pages. I shudder when I think of what the publication price is likely to be. The British publisher (Secker) said that he would import only 250 copies for Great Britain. How sad to think that only 250 people or institutions will want my book! But I shall at least have the great satisfaction of feeling that the book contains what I want it to contain, and some people will surely find it useful.

[. . .]

As ever,
Donald

NEW YORK, APRIL 3, 1984

Dear Shirley,

[. . .]

It seems like a long time since you left for Italy. Last week we had the worst storms of the winter, & today the full warmth of spring with only tattered piles of black snow here and there to remind us that there was a last week.

The term is going along slowly but not unpleasantly. A colleague has put the idea in my head of a brief sojourn in northern Italy towards the middle of May. I haven't been in France or Italy in almost twenty years. I have written to a friend at the University of Venice, where Japanese is taught, asking if they would like a lecture. This is not because I have anything special I wish to communicate to the Venetians about Japanese literature, but because I now feel embarrassed to be too recognizably a tourist.

Publication date of <u>Dawn to the West</u> has been set for April 30th. No doubt the publishers felt that it was a sense essential to give reviewers sufficient time to read the bulky volumes, but it means that I will not be here very long after publication. You have told me when you and Francis will return, but I can only remember that it is in April. I wish that New York had things to tempt you from Capri!

Last week I saw one such "thing"—a truly splendid performance of <u>Don Carlo</u>. It so rarely happens in the opera house that everything goes right, but this was one such occasion.

This weekend I shall be going to Dallas to give a talk at the new museum, when there is a large show of Japanese art at present.

[. . .]

I envy you the Italian spring. Here the sky is blue and the air is warm but there is hardly a bud to be detected. But come back soon, anyway! Yours, Donald

POSTCARD, KATHMANDU, MAY 31, 1984

Dear Shirley and Francis,

It seems like months, not just ten days ago, since we spoke on the telephone. Thank you for your "buon viaggio" message. From Venice we drove to Vienna, where I spent four absolutely delightful days trying, more or less in vain, to recall memories of the city which I last visited when I was nine. Only the bloodstained uniform of the archduke Franz Ferdinand had lingered in my memory. From Vienna, by a devious route to Kathmandu, where I have time on my hands despite the oriental and occidental (hippies) exoticism.

All my best, Donald

POSTCARD, NAPLES, JUNE 26, 1984

Thank you so much, dear Donald, for your astonishing card. Where will you be next, for heavens sake? (We hope "New York" is the answer to that question.) We are in full—& magnif.—summer here now, and rather appalled to be leaving—next week, for Florence & Siena; then NYC mid-July; then (for me) Australia, 1 Aug. (These lectures[8] are <u>killing</u> me.) Back in NYC around 24 Aug at latest. Italy in early Sept. sounds very jet-age (& quite frightening). We trust all well with you—I shan't even mention "work"—With love—Shirley.

TOKYO, JULY 9, 1984

Dear Shirley,

Thank you for your postcard with the Roman mural (and the big postage stamp with the Modigliani). I can imagine that leaving Capri for New York in July must be quite a wrench.

The book Francis asked me to have bound is ready, or almost. It has been bound in Japanese style, which means that it is rather like a box, rather than a leather binding. I hope that is what he meant. The title and the name of the author, which one expects that a binder in other countries would automatically supply, has been left blank. I asked the binder to write in the characters, but he refused, saying that he was unworthy of such a task. His father, who alas is dead, used to perform this service, but he himself had no such confidence in his calligraphy. I pointed out the unlikelihood that you or Francis would find fault with his calligraphy, but nothing I could say was of any use. So, I shall have to write the characters myself. I fear that you <u>will</u> be able to detect that something is not quite what it should be. If you find my writing objectionable it will be easy to paste another slip of paper over it and get someone with real calligraphic skills to oblige.

I have been waiting, with no results so far, for an invitation from the Editor-in-Chief to have a little chat about my journey to Europe this autumn. A comparative study of Vesuvius and Fuji. I have met the man in the hall and he promised that we would have a meeting someday, but it may be that he is not as enthusiastic about sending me abroad as I had been led to suppose. In any case, I shall be keeping my fingers crossed. I have been in Tokyo for over a month. I feel rather frustrated on several scores. First I have been having trouble adjusting to the very different kind of scholarship involved in reading ninth century poetry, after having spent so long on literature of the last hundred years. Second, for various unrelated reasons, I have been seeing much less of my Japanese friends than in the past. I dare not even phone them for fear my call will be interpreted as a reproach for not having kept in touch with me. (This may sound exaggerated, but Japanese tend to look behind every action for the real motives.) Third, my time seems to be eaten up by minor chores. After all these years I still have not learned how to say no.

You are obviously much more conscientious about preparing lectures than I. I hope that your audiences will be responsive. I enjoyed giving lectures in Australia except in Melbourne, where I had to start while the dessert and coffee were being served, and where I was told to shorten my lecture from 60 minutes to 30. But your lectures will no doubt be in a proper hall. I'm sure that they will create something of a sensation—but that will not be new for you.

All my best to you and Francis.
Yours, Donald

NEW YORK, JULY 14, 1984

Dear Donald—

A week ago today—today being le quatorze—we went on a lustral visit (it is, rather, a yearly or two-yearly one; but the purifying ritual is analogous) to an ancient deserted monastery in woods just outside Siena, a place reached only through a path overgrown with Sleeping Beauty vines and wild white roses. I knew it first nearly thirty years ago, when the "bestie" were still in the refectory, and the mangers & stalls obscured, perhaps not inappropriately, the holy frescoes— frescoes by Giovanni di Paolo. In the church there are frescoes by Lippo Vanni & other 14th c. Sienese. These have been restored, and the place put in 'order' about twenty years ago. There is a farmer who tends the place and acts as custode. So, in that silence—silence with birds and the hummings of the earth, of course—we arrived up the little slope to the church. Coming face to face with a woman in a mask, who asked us in American "What are you doing here? Are you just tourists?" in no cordial tones. Whereupon, a bevy or covy or platoon appeared out of a huge hole they had dug in the ground (searching for a mediaeval cistern; when it is found, they will fill it in again with earth and, thank God, go their ways). Villanova University. What was intimidating was their complete lack of interest in the natural and aesthetic meaning of the place, & their proprietary and indeed superior air. Only one spoke any Italian at all. Counterbalancing this, the contadino now acting as custodian, and his brother, turned out to be the farm-workers from my ancient Sienese days at a villa in the Chianti on the other side of Siena where I spent some part of each year for eight years—all now dead, sold, transformed etc. We recognised each other with joy, and leant on a stone wall in the sun talking about "the past", so beautiful, while figures in masks scurried past us. And, yes, at that villa of the past there actually was a cherry orchard; and it is now a swimming pool, I suppose.

I'm now getting ready, if that's the word, for Australia . . . Your letter gives hope that "They" will ask me to shorten <u>my</u> lectures from 60 mins to 30. Please press firmly on the Fuji-Vesuvio idea, we count on it. And don't forget the twin-city arrangement that exists between Kagashima and Naples (& the alternative Japanese menu at the Hotel Excelsior in Naples, a fruitful object of study).

I learn this (from Edgar Johnson's life of Dickens): that Ch. Dickens, aged eight, was occasionally taken to Theatre Royal near Chatham "and was inspired to compose a tragedy entitled MISNAR THE SULTAN OF INDIA (founded on one of the Tales of the Genii)." What are these Tales, I wonder?

So much to say. We miss your presence, recovered in your letter even if briefly. Shall keep in touch, & "report" on Aust . . .

With all affection—Shirley.

PS: As to not learning to say No—I agree that No is essential, & greatly suffer from inability to form that syllable. However, I just read an interview in VOGUE (USA) with a youngish woman novelist, M. Robinson, who teaches at Harvard, & says she urges her students not to squander their talents by being amusing in conversation, writing interesting letters or even postcards etc. God forbid one should find oneself at dinner with her. How mini-minded the world has become.

USAMI, AUGUST 15, 1984

Dear Shirley and Francis,

Thank you for your letter of le quatorze juillet. I have chosen another historic date for my reply. The 30th anniversary of the Japanese surrender. I'm writing this letter from my place on the Izu coast. It is a beautiful, hot summer day with great woolly cumulus clouds lazily drifting in a blue sky. Mishima loved these clouds, and I somehow have the feeling, certainly not received from him, that on the day of his death in November these summer clouds were in the sky. My penultimate sight of Mishima in 1970 was in this vicinity, in Shimoda, the town at the end of the Izu peninsula. (He came to the airport to see me off when I left for New York in September.) I keep thinking about him, about the kinds of books he might have written. I miss Mishima and Ivan most of all the people I have known who have died.

Thinking back to August 15, 1945, I recall the headquarters tent in Guam where I stood with three or four Japanese prisoners-of-war listening to the broadcast by the emperor announcing the end of the war. I could hardly understand anything of his high-pitched words. He was speaking in a remote, classical Japanese that I had never even studied. But when the prisoners burst into tears I knew what I had guessed, that the war, which I thought would never end, was in fact over. And now I write these lines looking out over a Bay with green hills on three sides, a little island and a big Island in the distance. I even own a couple of square meters of Japan, though I thought during the war it might evaporate at first touch. Outside a constant trilling of cicadas and in the sky two or three kites coasting in the air. I really have been very lucky.

I was delighted that you liked the "binding" of the Isadora Duncan book. Please let this be a present. [. . .]

I can't remember just when Shirley is to leave for Australia, but if she hasn't left yet, my best wishes for a pleasant journey & a wildly successful tour.

I have not had any encouragement concerning a trip to Europe in the autumn, but am still hoping.

Yours, Donald.

TOKYO, OCTOBER 18, 1984

Dear Shirley,

It was delightful to talk with you on the phone the other night (day?). I had tried so many times before I finally got through to your land-lady (?). She suggested that I telephone at 8:oo PM, but that would be 4:oo AM by my time, and I doubted that I would wake before then. I discovered that my Italian, limited at the best of times, was inadequate for what I wanted to say, but no sooner had I hung up that the words "domani a la stessa ora" flashed into my mind. I may have told you, I learned what Italian I know by listening to the Italian-speaking radio station in New York, and at the end of serials they always invited one to listen the next day at the same time. (I recall the opera hour especially. It was always introduced by the first part of Rosa Ponselle's recording of <u>Pace pace mio dio</u>, followed by the message from the sponsor, Pace pace mio dio olive oil.)

[. . .]

I plan to go from Rome to Capri after my arrival on November first. I probably will be tired, but not absolutely exhausted, and it will be restoring to see you, Francis and Elizabeth.

[. . .]

I look forward very much to seeing you again.

Yours, Donald

TOKYO, NOVEMBER 18, 1984

Dear Shirley and Francis,

It has been just a week since I returned to Tokyo. The day after my return I delivered a lecture in Gifu, a place about three hours journey from here, and yesterday I delivered a lecture in Yamagata, somewhat further away, on a totally unrelated subject. Tomorrow another lecture, and still another on Thursday, and then I shall have finished with lectures for the year. But rather than wait for that happy event, I want to write and thank you for a most delightful visit. It could not have been more enjoyable. [. . .]

The trip to Rome went smoothly. At the station a man standing by a yellow taxi invited me aboard his vehicle, but said, with hilarious honesty, that it would probably cost 25,000 lire to reach my hotel because of the heavy traffic. I realized then that there are yellow taxis and yellow taxis, and I noticed for the first time a long line of people waiting for the authentic yellow taxis. The hotel room was delightful, with a balcony. I wrote a note to the Meanas and delivered it with the aid of an Austrian who was studying yoga in the same building. I found my way to Papyrus and bought a box, had a splendid dinner at Otello, bought a chunk of Gorgonzola—in fact accomplished everything as planned and so carefully noted in Shirley's map.

I arrived the next day at the airport about two hours before the flight. I was informed that I was on a stand-by basis. I pointed out that I had a confirmed reservation and had reconfirmed. They admitted this was the case, but shrugged their shoulders when it came to doing something about it. I waited for an hour and began to get nervous. If I could not get aboard that particular flight I would miss my lecture in Gifu. Other people who were also on stand-by status began to be called, but my name did not come up. By now there was only half an hour until departure time. I providentially noticed at this point a Japanese employee of Alitalia and poured out my griefs to him. He fortunately had heard of me, and he did everything conceivable to get me aboard. Ten minutes before departure time he appeared with a ticket and I trampled several people under foot in my eagerness to get on the bus. The seat was in business class, much nicer than my usual economy class, but it took several hours before the agitation subsided.

[. . .]

The radio is playing <u>Cosi Fan Tutte</u> in the background. It is terrible to have such glorious music in one's ears and not to listen properly, but I simply cannot put off writing you another day to say thank you once again for a truly wonderful ten days. Yours always, Donald

NEW YORK, DECEMBER 18, 1984

Dear Donald—

Thank you so much for your letter. I'm answering at once so that you will have some responses—even if unsatisfactory ones—to yr Neapolitan questions. [. . .]

The frescoes at the Liceo are described as follows in the Guida Rosa (Touring Club Italiano guide)—my translation:

ex-Oratorio dei Nobili, at one time part of the complex of the adjacent Church of the GESÙ NUOVO, and now gymnasium of the Liceo 'A. Genovesi': two vast rooms, the first frescoed with SAINTS AND ALLEGORIES by Giovanni Lanfranco, the decoration being arranged around a central group of the NATIVITY by Giovanni Battósta Caracciolo; the second is painted with SCENES OF THE LIFE OF MARY by an unknown painter of the 18th century.

Gesù Nuovo, by the way, simply designates the fact that the church was consecrated after the first "church of Gesù" at Naples (a very ancient edifice, now enclosed within the university). "A Genovesi" is the name of the person who is being honoured by a liceo in his name (like "Martin Luther King High School"). Lanfranco and "Battistiello" Carraciolo are two of the finest Neapolitan 17th century painters—well represented at the show we saw.

Delighted to think all this will be commemorated in Japanese. [. . .] The first set of frescoes are of course mixed classical and Christian scenes. The church you and I went into in the evening is San Pietro a Maiella (the St Peter in this case deriving from a mountain in southern Italy called the Maiella) and is the church adjoining and belonging to the Conservatory of Music (Beethoven glowering, as well he might, in courtyard).

[. . .]

Word processor, not for us. My only hope of getting anything "right" is to have to correct it myself rather than by machine. The threat of an eraser "concentrates one's mind wonderfully".

Schubert—what a miracle—unbearable—beautiful.

We look forward to Jan 15. Francis may "have" to go to Paris for a week at New Year—to see a huge Diderot show, about which he may write. Otherwise—we are here, eagerly waiting our reunion.

With all affection—Shirley.

TOKYO, JUNE 16, 1985

Dear Shirley,

It has been just a week since I returned to Tokyo. I'm now not only re-established in my Tokyo domicile but have resumed the rather hectic life here that contrasts so with my New York life. For you Capri is the quiet part of your year; for me New York is much quieter than Tokyo!

Everything went smoothly in Rome thanks to your kind help. The Hotel d'Inghilterre, which to the end seems not to have heard from my travel agent, had the room which you secured for me. [. . .] The next morning, with your instructions in hand, I set out sightseeing.

I normally have the capacity to get lost no matter how carefully I am directed, but your instructions were a miracle of clarity. I looked in the Pantheon and inspected Raphael's tomb, then went on to the Church of San Luigi dei Francisi. What a superb church! The Caravaggio chapel was of course magnificent. As I write I'm looking at a postcard of the painting to the left, "Vocasione di S. Matteo". It seems to me a more memorable picture than any in the Caravaggio show I saw in New York. What a painter! Shuffling my postcards, I see now one of "Madonna dei pellegrini" which I saw at the Chiesa di S-Agostino. Another superb painting in an unforgettable church. I thought that I knew Rome fairly well, though my knowledge is restricted to the years 1950–1953, but I think it is likely I have never visited either church. Is it possible? Or could I have forgotten?

I visited also the Biblioteca Angelica, murmuring the password which you taught me, and was delighted. I think that during my next visit to Italy I must spend more time in Rome, though I enjoy the sensation of "discovering" Naples under your aegis, and the perfection of a place like Lucca is hard to match.

Emboldened by my success in seeing the various sites you guided me to, I managed on my own to walk to Castel San Angelo. That building always stirs me both by itself and by its associations with Tosca, and beyond that with the sad stories of the many men who were imprisoned there. I can't remember if I have told you of my friend in England, Mrs Dickins, who translated the letters of Settembrini, who spent much of his life in prison. She never found a publisher, perhaps because she was always sure that her work would be rejected.

And, of course, I must thank you again for Capri. I remember best the moonrise as we sat dining near the Natural Arch, swimming between the Faraglioni, lunch by the water with fish swarming in the clear water and, of course, the dinners at the fabled Gemma's. I can understand enough Italian to have been able to follow your conversation with the man who made Xerox copies for you: you said that Capri was a paradise, and he agreed. So do I.

In a week or so I shall be making a trip in order to write an article for the NY Times. I was given complete freedom and I suppose I could write without going to the Inland Sea again, but it is a good occasion. I may have told you, but a Kabuki theatre about 200 years old has been perfectly restored and there are to be performances there beginning on the 26th of June. It may be uncomfortable sitting Japanese style through a whole morning and afternoon (no artificial lighting, I gather), But it will be worth it, even if I can't find a place in my article for the play.

All my best wishes to you and Francis. Yours, Donald

CAPRI, JUNE 29, 1985

Dear Donald—

[. . .]

Donald, you are the most delightful person in the world to propose excursions to (and in so many other ways). You not only <u>do</u> the things suggested, but you actually enjoy them—surely you must yourself have had those reports, from your own visitors, of the difficulties encountered in following your proposals, or the disappointing nature of the monuments when finally reached over a multiplicity of obstacles . . . You, instead, seem to find the destination with perfect ease, and to find nothing anti-climactic about, say, Caravaggio's series on San Matteo. John Pope-Hennessy did in fact try to pry those pictures loose from San Luigi dei F. for the Metropolitan's Caravaggio show—I thought this rather outrageous, and was relieved when the loan was refused. Magnificent, aren't they? And so "involved", in the old use of that word, so complex in the composition and execution. As to the Metrop. Exhibition, I do think that Flagellation tremendous—the brute enjoyment of the floggers, the reduction and passivity of the victim. In the exhibition that came to Washington, having opened at the Royal Academy, some years ago (the adapted and in a sense enlarged version of which you saw last year at Capodimonte), the great Naples picture, "The Seven Works of Charity", was included and it is now at the Capodimonte show of Caravaggio which closes today. But it had been travelling for years, is of immense value in all senses, and was so long unseen at Naples that the Beni Culturali would not lend it again for the Metropolitan Caravaggio show this year. You will see it when you next come to Naples.

How splendid that you went into Sant-Agostino, <u>and</u> into the Angelica library. The moment of entering that library is one which never fails to astonish and delight, a sensation of discovery, I think. And then—that you went to Castel Sant-Angelo all in that morning—what a wonderful place. Those upper rooms, decorated by Perin del Vaga for Pope Paul III, seem to me a sort of splendid dream. One comes out on to the terrace afterwards in a daze of pleasure.

[…]

I wonder what became of the manuscript of Mrs. Dickins' Settembrini letters?

[…]

At the Arco Naturale I have told them of your writing from Tokyo to "remember best" the moonrise on the evening of our dinner there. This evening Francis and I hope to see it again. Will you ever forget that sudden red apparition, and the silence that fell on the diners in those moments? One of the beauties of Capri is as you say that, while swimming in its sea, one can look up and see the Faraglioni or the limestone cliffs or the Monte Solaro right overhead. Enough to make a Xerox operator feel he is in paradise. I have so many things to tell you of life since then—but when we meet would like especially to describe a little our days visiting the Ville Vesuviane recently.

Good heavens. Naples is always turning on not just something more or something unexpected but a positive Vesuvius of erupting astonishments and pleasures. [. . .]

We look forward to the Inland Sea results, and the Kabuki report. And to hearing from you when you have time—and of course to seeing you as soon as possible. Thank you for your beautiful box, on which Francis's eye at once fell, and which he too enjoys handling for its sympathetic "feel" and fineness. And for the as yet intact Panforte, which we will open on F's birthday next week. He was extremely sorry to miss you here, and has enjoyed hearing about it all, and thinking that you'll visit Capri again before long.

With warm affection from us both—Shirley.
PS: If my directions are lucid, as you kindly say, it's because I try to imagine myself following them and thus reduce all concepts to infantile possibilities susceptible of realisation by a directionless person like myself. Neither F nor I has innate sense of "place".

TOKYO, JULY 29, 1985

Dear Shirley,

I was very pleased to receive your letter, the delightful contents of which were presaged by the beautiful postage stamps on the envelope. I was also much interested in the article from the Italian newspaper which brought me a new word, <u>yamatologo</u>, a variation no doubt on the more familiar Japanologue. The book you said you had not heard of, the collection of essays dedicated to Ivan Morris, was based on a plan he had to devote a whole book in English to one chapter of <u>The Tale of Genji</u>, the chapter being the one called "Ukifune". I remember that he asked me to participate, but the period was so remote from what I was working on then (though close to what I'm working on now) that I declined. Ivan planned to make a literal (as literal as one can make a translation from Japanese into English) version and also one into his usual elegant style; but all that he left at the time of his death was the literal one, and the editor (a former student, now the director of the Asia House Gallery) decided for reasons not known to me not to include it in the book.

[. . .]

Next month a Japanese group of singers are to perform Mascagni's opera <u>Iris</u>. I know one aria, recorded by Gigli a long time ago, but I have never taken it seriously if only because two of the principal characters are known as Osaka and Kyoto. Surely <u>somebody</u> could have told poor Mascagni that people and cities don't necessarily have the same names. It's something to look forward to—the Japanese performing a work of <u>japonaiserie</u>, trying to act as quaintly as possible while roaring out verismo arias.

Your mention of Mr Casaubon in your letter reminded me that I had a copy of <u>Adam Bede</u> which I had bought for the plane but not yet read. I have started it. I find George Eliot a most impressive writer. This is certainly no startling discovery. But the last two English 19th century novels I read (<u>The Egoist</u> of George Meredith and <u>Barchester Towers</u>) made me wonder if Japanese literature hadn't disqualified me as an appreciator of late Victorian fiction. But George Eliot has reassured me. I have also read recently with enormous interest the diaries of Alice James.

My best to you and Francis. Yours, Donald

TOKYO, JUNE 23, 1986

Dear Shirley and Francis,

I have been meaning to write you ever since my return to Tokyo last Sunday, but I have been stopped by a curious problem: I still have not found the answer to the entirely reasonable question Shirley asked about where enemy aliens were kept during the war. I have received various answers, such as, "They were all exchanged with Japanese who had been living abroad," or "They continued to live where they were but under police surveillance." Recently a man promised to ask someone who was formerly in the military police and knows about such matters, but I'm still waiting for a reply. One place is sometimes named, Karuizawa in the mountains. I know that some foreigners, notably Germans, spent the war years there, and perhaps enemy aliens also resided in that remote town. I used to know a Belgian priest who was interned, and he certainly could provide an answer, but I don't know where he is at present. Anyway, I haven't forgotten. I shall write again as soon as I retain some information.

So many pleasant things happened from the time I met you in Capri. After that I went, as you know, to Milan where I stayed with my friends. I saw the famous churches in the city (including San Eustorgio), the Brera, the small but excellent Poldi Pezzoli Museum, and the Charterhouse at Pavia. Best of all, perhaps, was a performance at La Scala of <u>Pélleas et Mélisande</u> conducted by Abbado. The only outstanding singer was the American Frederika von Stade, but I have never before been so moved by the flow of the music. The sets were also excellent, especially one that depicted the interior of the well into which the lovers look, their heads just showing above the parapet looking down.

The week in Egypt was superb despite the incredible heat in Upper Egypt (45 degrees in the shade, 57 degrees in the sun). Unlike my dreary experience in Finland, the people at the Japanese embassy did everything humanly possible to make the stay memorable, and they certainly succeeded.

And now back to Tokyo, which seems the antithesis of exotic. There are many requests for lectures, all highly paid and difficult to refuse. There are equal numbers of requests for manuscripts, and I really will have to think up ways of saying no.

[. . .] Milan struck me as being the most elegant city I have ever visited, though naturally I saw only the best parts. But I'm much more strongly drawn to Naples with its ruined palaces than to the polish of Milan. I haven't yet decided what to do about the offered job at the University of Naples. If only I could swallow a magic pill and be able to speak and understand Italian! That would decide me, but I am afraid that learning Italian would mean irregular verbs, subjunctives, and all the rest. I feel too old to get involved with la plume de ma tante again.

Thank you again for the delightful stay in Capri in Naples. I'm afraid that my changes of plan must have proved a nuisance & a hindrance to your work, but I was really pleased to visit your new place in Naples. Yours, Donald

CAPRI AND NAPLES, JULY 20, 1986

Dear Donald—

I feel shame at this delay in answering your so kind letter, and your postcard. Our lives since we last saw you have been of the benevolent treadmill kind, and the usual effect—never having repose to writing a letter one really cares about—has not been lacking. [. . .]

What I regret of your stay is—well, such things as not having managed to take you into our landlords' villa and down to the sea below. Not getting to the Archaeological Museum, or to San Martino; or to a performance of music. And so on. But we remember so many things with pleasure that perhaps these deficiencies—which we'll remedy next time—or hope to—are not too glaring? I think your Milan stay was a good one, from your report of it? Yes, how delightful the Poldo-Pezzoli. Alone in Milan on my first visit there, on a wintry day in late 1957, I remember being made really happy there. Seeing that small Guardi for the first time would be enough to make anyone happy, I shld think—the "Laguna Grigia".

[. . .]

I used to think it strange that Milan was for so long the imperial capital and yet had (with some eminent exceptions) so little of Roman monuments in it—as the late empire was a time of much building. Since reading Gibbon, and suffering through the numbers of times that Milan, as capital, was razed by Huns, Goths, etc etc, I'm surprised that anything at all is left. If you haven't done so, some day you must visit Aosta in its stupendous valley (which leads to the Mont Blanc tunnel more or less directly). The city and its countryside give an overwhelming feeling of the Roman presence—the departures for the Alps, and the returns. It is full of Roman constructions. A beautiful place, which we used to drive through in late autumn going from Florence to Geneva years ago—a wonderful time to see it, as in late Oct the vineyards (terraced high into the mountainsides) are red, and the grapes in that cool place are still being picked.

I think that anyone who has learned Japanese need have no fear of the Italian subjunctive either past or present.

There is so much to say and yet it is mostly of a Neapolitan kind—experiences of sights and lights [. . .], and—as at the Arco Naturale—the phenomenon Auden described in this gulf as finding in a vista "an absolute goal." We have used your Finnish pale wooden "mat" rather extravagantly often, and admired it every time. "Our" woodworker ("falegname"), who has been doing various jobs in our place at Naples, took much pleasure in handling and examining it, and noted the northern woods, blond and seldom "profondi". [. . .]

Now we're at Naples. I even forget what interrupted me as I was writing to you from Capri—it would stun me if I were _not_ interrupted. This evening the gulf is oddly in relief, like an old photograph. A cool wind, after very hot days. This morning we sat out under a tree in the garden—on the park side of the house—and read about the fall of Alexandria to the Moslems. A most thrilling and appalling section of Gibbon, this Mohammedan part, recounted with his customary high style and imperturbable genius.

On F's eightieth birthday we were reunited with Graham Greene on Capri—that is, we had the pleasantest time with him we've had in many years. [. . .] He would like me to devote my days and years to the Waldheim case,[9] but I don't fancy spending the rest of my life with a snake. I wonder whether there is any interest, or any general understanding of the issues, in this story in Japan? Japanese have had so much of their own trouble in that line, they may not have energy left over for the Viennese variety. Thank you for keeping after my interests in the Japanese prison that would have harboured civilian political prisoners of other nationalities, particularly of belligerent nationals who declared themselves anti-axis. If we could find out where Fosco Maraini was imprisoned, would that not be an answer of a kind? Can I some time ask you a handful of other immediate post-war Japanese questions, as I come to them in my writing? I'd be grateful.

[. . .]

With all friendliest greetings from us both, and with much affection—Shirley.

TOKYO, SEPTEMBER 5, 1986

Dear Shirley,

Now it is my turn to feel ashamed of a long silence. It is not that I have let you and Francis drift out of my thoughts. I have been putting off an answer until I was able to answer your question about the place where nonmilitary enemy aliens were interned during the war. The question should be easy to answer. There are undoubtedly many people who actually had the experience and could tell me if I knew how to get in touch with them. But, believe it or not, I'm still unable to give you a clear answer. Most Japanese assume that enemy aliens were repatriated in 1942 on the first or second ship (Gripsholm, I think). I have been told that those who remained were interned in Karuizawa or Hakone, two mountain resorts. I <u>know</u> that Germans were in Karuizawa during the war. But they were not enemies. I bought a book by an elderly Australian named Harold S Williams called <u>Tales of the Foreign Settlements in Japan</u>. It is maddening: he writes as if he knew what specifically I wanted to learn and was deliberately refusing to tell me. On page 24 there is this statement: "Mr. Griffiths died during the war in the Canadian Academy Internment Camp." Mr. Griffiths <u>seems</u> to have been an Australian (Williams never says). He lived in Kobe, which is where the Canadian Academy still is. I telephoned a friend who is a member of the board of directors of the academy and asked if he knew whether or not it was a place of internment for foreigners during the war, but he had never heard anything to that effect. He suggested I try the police!

I don't know why you need this information. Presumably you want to be accurate about some detail in the novel you are writing. I think that if you say the camp was in Karuizawa or Hakone, nobody will object (unless a survivor, who has been waiting for a chance to denounce irresponsible novelists, decides to write a letter to the Editor of the TLS). If you give Kobe, this may be a mistake, but you can blame Mr. Williams. He was born in 1898, so he probably has learned by this time how to defend himself.

Peter Morton sent me the tapes of a series of broadcasts about Japan with which he had some connection. They are intelligently organized, and the technical problem of what to do with Japanese who do not speak English has been cleverly solved. But the series is so distorted politically that I find it painful to listen to the tapes. I imagine that the series is intended as a look at Japan from the other side, in contrast to the familiar explanations of Japan's economic miracle, the harmony in factories, lifetime employment and so on. But the Japanese speakers are all extremely left-wing members of the new left, and some of what they say is plainly untrue. For example, we are told that the farmers are so oppressed and have such difficulty making a living from the soil that most of them must also work elsewhere in order to make ends meet. It is true that there are now only some 100,000 Japanese who make a living exclusively from agriculture, but this is because the use of farm machinery has drastically reduced the number of hours they must work on the land, and enabled them to augment their already considerable incomes by taking other jobs. Most farmers now consider themselves middle-class, and many have been to Europe. The prostitutes in Copenhagen are said to know one Japanese word, "Nōkyō", the abbreviation of "Farmers' Union"; they greet Japanese with this word, assuming that they are members of the union! Anyway, this makes it very difficult for me to thank Peter Morton, whom I liked very much when we met.

I have written to the professor of Japanese in Naples saying that I would like to teach there in the spring of 1988. I don't expect an answer for some time, considering how long it is likely for anything official to be arranged, but I have formally requested permission from Columbia Univ to be on leave during that spring. This coming spring is not possible because colleagues are on leave, and I would prefer to have my stay in Naples and environs during the spring, when there is much music, rather than in the autumn.

To answer your question: I have not seen any expression of Japanese interest in the Waldheim case, though I might easily have missed articles in the serious magazines. The Japanese tend to be unreservedly in favor of anything international, at least in principle, perhaps by way of reaction to wartime nationalism. Please do ask any questions you may have about Japan, but my knowledge of the immediate post war situation is second-hand. All my best to you and Francis. Yours Donald

POSTCARD, NAPLES, SEPTEMBER 20, 1986

Dear Donald—

Your letter of 5 September just reached me, brought here by Francis from NY—he arrived yesterday—and I send an interim quick word to thank you. I was just going to write you, in case you'd not been well. Thank you, you've answered my Japanese internment question—it's all I need. Yes, of course, that survivor who has been waiting his opportunity forty years will certainly pounce. Good news, great news, that you've requested a spell of teaching at Naples in 88 (a year when I've been asked to go to Australia for the bicentennial—probably in August if I accept). I hope indeed you will write to Peter Morton what you've written me about those tapes—how otherwise will he know the truth?—he is a "liberal" (small l), but very objective and not at all in favour of distorting the political reality for a particular end. He really must be told about the nature of these broadcasts . . .

Radiant days here—& in Capri—tonight we are the only people not going to hear Bernstein conduct at Pompeii—all affection from us both—Shirley.

TOKYO, OCTOBER 17, 1986

Dear Shirley,

Thank you for your card with the picture of the Marina Grande. It brought back fond memories of Capri. I have trouble remembering where you are, especially now that there are three places where you might be. I hope that this letter is being sent to the right place.

I wrote Peter Morton, as you suggested. I realized that it is difficult for me to accept the views of certain Japanese, though I might accept them if voiced by people of some other nationality. When I was first living in Japan in the 1950s there was a strong anti-American bias to almost everything written in intellectual magazines. Some of the accusations were in fact quite correct. I had myself had more than once made up my mind not to return to America. (I was teaching at Cambridge until just before I went to Japan.) The McCarthy era deserved to be attacked. But there was always the fear on my part that if the anti-American writers had their way all Americans, including myself of course, would have to leave the country and never return. Examined objectively, there was little reason for me to be so alarmed. The mass of the Japanese people was not anti-American, those writers who seemed most hostile probably did not have in mind forcible ejection of all Americans. But the thought that I might not be able to return was so painful that every sign of hostility frightened me. I suppose that something of this fear still lingers, so even the intellectuals today have been so disillusioned with respect to the USSR and China that there is no longer a model to adopt in place of America. Probably the greatest danger now, even to me personally, is not from the far left but from the right. The recent utterances of Nakasone and members of his cabinet and especially the revival of official worship at the Yasukuni Shrine seem to signal a new nationalism. So far, this nationalism is not directed against any country, but is content with insisting on the uniqueness and superiority of Japanese civilization. I remember the things I read during the war; there is much repetition. But, on the other hand, when I heard on Peter Morton's tapes the same kind of utterances I used to hear in the 1950s and early 1960s I felt the same pain I did at that time.

[...]

Today is the first of autumnal weather. I'm flying tonight to a town in northern Japan where there may even be snow. Ugh. I have become much in demand as a speaker, and though I refuse whenever I can, I seem somehow to accept even more. This whole month will be frittered away in lectures. I will end up with a lot of money, but the only thing I really want to buy is time, and that is precisely what I am squandering.

I trust that all goes well with you and Francis. When will you be back in New York? I hope you will be there in January when I return. Yours, Donald

CAPRI, NOVEMBER 4, 1986

Dear Donald—

Thank you so much for yr letter of 17 Oct, which just reached us in Capri. [. . .] This autumn in Italy has been the most radiant such season I recall since the autumn of 1969, which gave us—we were then in Tuscany—just these same warm and golden days. Until the thunderstorms of the last 48 hours, we have not only lunched but dined outdoors almost every day, and worn summer clothes. The Capresi are still swimming—their only chance, as they are too busy in the summer; the winter is only signalled by the very early dark, and by the blessedly bleak piazza and closed shops and hotels.

I'm glad you wrote to Peter Morton. But, in your present letter, you make—I think—quite different points about his broadcast from before, and I realise that anti-Americanism was one of its themes. Previously you'd written about the distortions of the changes in agricultural communities in Japan. As to anti-Americanism, I don't know what to say. I have many thoughts about this and its role in world terror. There is of course an entity named America, and its government is—I believe—behaving in a calamitous and tyrannical way to nations that do not give servile assent to its demands. We perhaps never thought to see this. It is not only the savagery against Viet Nam or Central America, or the maintaining in power of brutal regimes like that of the colonels in Greece, or Argentina, of Pinochet, or of Marcos until they fall of their own corruption. It is the rage against, say, New Zealand for taking a stand on principle; or against Aquino for not putting "communists" to fire and sword. I hardly think all this can be condemned enough, and most Americans we know (who are so small a fraction of "the American people", but who are in positions to be heard and perhaps to influence events at times) do so vehemently on their own ground. As soon as they go abroad, this seems to fall to pieces; they remember not only the better aspects of their nation, but forget what harm is being done. They also, more reasonably, resent the offensiveness—which, in a country like Australia is often a personal animosity disguised, thinly, as concern for world politics—with which criticisms are directed at themselves as representatives of such a country; and, underneath, I think, there is a sense that many many people are getting even if unconsciously a lot of mileage out of "hating" America; just as people who say they "hate Germans" have often merely found an object at which to direct meaningless hatred that is in themselves. None of this changes the fact that "America" has invited hatred and criticism. My own feeling is that there is no hope for a change in world hostility until there is some realisation around the globe that there are people in every country who are generally speaking merely trapped in the fact of being born into one nationality or another; and who feel kinship with all signs of reason and pity around the world, before all else. Whose nationality, that is, is incidental to them; or minor in comparison with being a member of the human race. Many people would claim to subscribe to this idea, I believe; but rarely does one find it genuinely put into practice.

Even I have been able to see these signals of Japanese nationalism, from my small reading in such matters. Nationalism—tribalism—is on the rise around the globe in a frightening and swift spiral. Italy remains clear of it so far, and Naples would laugh at the idea. This is in part, as Lily once said to me, because someone tried to generate it here recently with such appalling results: "Abbiamo avuto una tale indigestione . . ."[10]

[. . .]

We felt so much your remarks about lecturing, and time. "What I really want to buy is time", you say. Yes, not only time to write, but time for the state of mind and thought; time for prolonged and habitual silences.

[. . .]

On the 14th we go to Venice for a few days. On about 23 Nov to NYC. Of course we'll be looking for news of your January return, and hoping for word meantime. With much affection as ever—Shirley.

TOKYO, NOVEMBER 25, 1986

Dear Shirley,

Thank you very much for your letter of 4 November. It made me want to answer immediately, but I restrained myself, remembering that you have other things to do besides correspond with me.

[. . .]

I had a very nice letter from Peter Morton saying that my letter had been discussed by the people directly responsible for preparing the program that I had so disliked. I misled you in suggesting it was anti-American. Or if it was anti-American and nothing more it wouldn't have bothered me at this stage. No, the program was neither anti-American nor pro-Soviet nor anything of that kind. The Japanese left has become disillusioned with its former idols and now contents itself mainly with attacking Japan. There is certainly much that is wrong in this country, as I suppose in any country; but what offended me was not attacking but falsification. I gave the instance of agriculture because it is easiest to demonstrate that it is factually wrong. But when it pictures all Japanese unions as being in the pay of the employers, it is harder to show that this is not the case. And when they take up something which is true, but magnify it to such proportions that it ceases to be true, it is even harder to draw the line between permissible exaggeration for the sake of rhetorical effectiveness and outright lying. It is quite true, for example, that there is a class which still is subject to discrimination. Nobody knows why this is so, but it has been true for centuries. It disgusted me when I learned of it. But it is wrong to insist on this without making it clear that the amount and kind of discrimination have been enormously reduced in recent years. Probably a large part of the Japanese population is now unaware even of the existence of the problem. But the broadcast made it seem as if the worst of Nazi racism was being practiced in Japan.

I agree with you, of course. The fact of having been born in a particular country should have no more effect on one's attitudes than of having been born in a particular city. No one would persecute or defame another person just because of the city he was born in. I wrote an article for a Japanese magazine in which I said the only hope for mankind was rootless cosmopolitanism, choosing the term Hitler had used.[11] A book of essays in Japanese will be published in January with a title something like "Living in Two Motherlands". I hope that startles people.

Yesterday I had bad news. The professor in Naples who had invited me to teach at his university dropped dead of a heart attack at the age of 41. Incredible. I don't think he had been ill previously; must have been very sudden. I did not know him well, but we had a delightful half-day together in Rome. I assume that this means that I shall not be invited to Naples, but the friend who informed me of this sad event is now waiting for word as to whether or not he has been appointed a professor of Japanese art at the University of Genoa. He intends to invite me there if he is. Of course, it would not be impossible to go to Italy quite unaided, and I would like to do so in 1988 when I shall be taking leave from Columbia. But I must think of some way of manifesting myself only when you and Francis have nothing else to do. I fear that I have taken up too much precious time. Perhaps Francis has run across a 17th century abbé who was fascinated by Japan. Unlikely. Anyway, if you refuse to surround yourself with defensive works I shall have to build them for you, allowing you to come out only when I am quite sure that you really need a rest from your labors.

[. . .] I am reading now a big book called <u>The Last Prima Donnas</u> by a man called Rasponi. I was startled when reading the chapter on Ebe Stignali, the great mezzosoprano of the postwar years, to discover she had been trained at the Conservatory of San Pietro di Maiella, as had Maria Caniglia, another singer I remember. No doubt there is such a Conservatory, but my impression of the church was that its peace and quiet was rarely disturbed by singers or pianists practicing scales.

I expect to be back in New York sometime after the tenth of January. I am delighted that you and Francis will be there.

Yours, Donald

CARD, NEW YORK, DECEMBER 1, 1986

Dear Donald—

Your extremely welcome letter just came, and—showing none of the thoughtful restraint you yourself display regarding immediate correspondence, I send you my first Christmas message of the year, perhaps not inappropriately inscribed on the reverse of the Pantheon. [. . .]

How shocking, the death of your colleague at Naples. What moments these are, when one realises the fragility of the thread— then one goes on as if Damocles had no part in one's day. Please let us know what results at Genova—and how interesting that there should be a department of Japanese art there. Yesterday I had a call from our friend Peter Morton—about an invitation to me to visit Australia in 1988 (their bicentennial year). I simply cannot commit myself to this generous idea at present, as I'm in a panic about my time lost, this year, on my ms, and we'll talk again about it in the new year. [. . .]

You will have seen what's going on in the USA—I suppose this Iranian affair is one of a thousand such shockers the Reagan administration has in hand. Even if Reagan were disgraced over it, on the analogy of Nixon, the public appears to learn nothing, merely going on to elect the next patent imbecile or malefactor.

I think we went together into the music conservatory?—It is next door to that great Church of San Pietro a Maiella—a huge series of cloisters, the religious establishment long since transformed into a musical one. Do you not recall an anguished seated statue of Beethoven in the first cloister, peering out from a scaffolding of repairs? Lanfranco Rasponi (who may, I think, have died a couple of years ago) is a curious case—a man who truly loved opera and knew much, but a person made absurd in company by his preposterous snobbery and talk of his lineal descent, his palazzi, etc . . . San P. a Maiella is the centre of musical training & scholarship at Naples— there is also a delightful museum there of musical instruments.

Just back—severely culturally shocked and appalled by the cold, but having some nice times with friends. So much to think about from our Italian months—we had a most beautiful week in Venice in mid-November. More of all this when we meet in mid-January. We're greatly looking forward to that reunion—with best affection, and our greatest greetings for Christmas and this new year—Shirley

TOKYO, DECEMBER 13, 1986

Dear Shirley,

Your Christmas letter was so good that I cannot resist answering it, even though a soft voice within me keeps whispering that even reading a letter will take you from your work.

I enjoyed the picture of the Pantheon, recalling one of my whirlwind morning tours of Rome under your aegis. I had forgotten the obelisk in front. Either I am losing my memory or I am plain unobservant: I had forgotten the statue of Beethoven at the music conservatory next to San Pietro a Maiella. My memory of the church itself, however, is absolutely clear. No, not clear—how could it be in semi-darkness?—but whole. The long shadows, the sound of the priest's voice, the echoing of our own footsteps—quite unforgettable. Perhaps (I am trying to defend my memory) we didn't actually go into the music school. [. . .]

The situation in America, seem from this distance, is appalling. Probably it is worse closer to the events. The thought of (1) selling arms to the Iranians and (2) using the proceeds for the enemies of the régime we recognize in Nicaragua is more than I can understand. Perhaps the people who are actually involved think of it as some kind of game, with extra points awarded for absolutely baffling actions. Reagan's popularity, even with people who suffer from the effects of his policies, is equally baffling. What has taken the place of self-interest, I wonder? The strangest thing of all is that in a country with 200 million people it is not possible to find a better president.

I'm reading some wonderful diaries now, kept by a man who in the 1850s and 1860s travelled extensively in the northern island of Hokkaidō. His account of the Ainu, the aboriginal inhabitants, in some ways recalls the accounts of Indians in America and perhaps the aborigines in Australia. But the fascinating thing is that this man goes out of his way to report every instance known to him of injustice dealt the Ainu by the Japanese. It is extraordinary that anyone at that time could have adopted a viewpoint that seems much more typical of the 1960s or later. I'm thinking of the films now being made in which the Indians are the victims and perhaps the heroes too. I've become quite excited about this man, whose name was unknown to me until less than a month ago.

I look forward to seeing you and Francis again. [. . .]

Yours, Donald

2

1987–1996

TOKYO, JULY 10, 1987

Dear Shirley,

What a long time it has been since we were last in touch! I have often thought of writing, but I feared that my letter might interrupt you just when the end of the novel was in sight or something equally dramatic was about to occur. I still have these feelings, knowing that you would write if you were not in the midst of important work or (perish the thought!) if you were not being besieged by visitors.

The answer to this letter can be very brief. In fact it can be in one word, if that is all you have time for. I believe I mentioned to you that I gave three lectures at the New York Public Library last year. I gave another at the Metropolitan Museum this past spring. An editor from Columbia University Press heard one or more of these talks and asked to see the manuscript. I've now been informed that (for reasons I do not understand) they are giving this book special priority and rushing it into print. This is very gratifying, but I'm a little nervous. The book is really not anything startlingly new but rather in the nature of musings on different aspects of traditional Japanese literature. [. . .] I thought I would like to dedicate the book to you and

Francis. May I have your permission? (Needless to say, you are under no obligation to read it, even if you graciously give consent!)

My plans for travel aren't yet clear, but I expect to go to Paris about the 20th of September for a conference to be held between French and American scholars of East Asia. I should probably go to Belgium after that. The Japanese friend is now the ambassador there, and he said he would try to arrange a lecture for me at Louvain. I will then go back to Japan because I have a lecture engagement there that I cannot break. Then to Venice about October 12 for a three-day session. If you will be in southern Italy at this time, and if you have the time to spare, I would be happy to visit you for a short time. There are two other possibilities of going to Europe. One is to visit various institutions where Japanese culture is taught, the other is to attend a meeting to be held at the former Japanese Embassy in Berlin, which after forty years as a bomb-scarred shell has been rebuilt as a center of Japanese culture. Finally, my friend in Milan has indirectly let me know that he is arranging lectures for me in Italy in late March.

This is a great deal of travelling at a time when I really should be consecrating myself to completing my history. I'm not sure that I will in fact be doing all of the above.

I may have told you that I joined a new institute for Japanese culture. I am officially a Japanese civil servant! I was so intrigued by the possibility that I did not stop to consider the possible disagreeable aspects of this new role. The people at the institute are all very kind, but the government officials, who know every regulation and precedent by heart, have made me regret this step. It is only for a year, if I can survive the repeated pinpricks that long.

[. . .]

I will be pleased to hear from you, if only on the matter of the dedication.

Yours, Donald

NEW YORK, AUGUST 22, 1987

Dear Donald—

We greatly hope that by now you have our cable, sent in response to your post card received yesterday. We are honoured and delighted to accept your dedication, and only hope to deserve it. Of course we had not had your letter to Capri (and I really don't understand why it was not "forwarded back" to New York. [. . .] The Italian mails are now virtually closed down in August—as, to an increasing extent, are those in the USA. However it may be, we had much pleasure in receiving your card, and only regretted you'd been so long without our response to this friendliest of gestures.

[. . .]

It has been a summer of some losses—including that of our Neapolitan friend Roberto Pane, who suddenly died at the end of July. He was ninety years old, but so hyper-active, and so full of work and planned volumes, that his end was utterly unexpected. He died after a peculiarly strenuous day passed in crisscrossing the gulf of Naples (for various undertakings) in heat of 100°. He was formidable, irreplaceable—and of course is now receiving in the press the tributes withheld from him in life. His immense body of revelatory work is his monument; but his personality too was of a kind, and quality, that one now rather thinks of as extinct—fearless, polymathic, hugely energetic, and entirely without hypocrisy. In an interview earlier this year, on his ninetieth birthday, he was asked his own choice of his most important quality, and gave the answer: "Coerenza"—which, in the Italian sense, means consistency and a sort of integrity of persistence (as well as having our own sense, clarity). He also said, of his life's dedication to the art and architecture not only of South Italy but of, in a way, all the world, "I will defend with my last breath the memory of the human past."

[. . .] We have had many beautiful days and weeks this spring and summer; although July and August have been months of particularly ferocious heat on both sides of the Atlantic. Capri is never intolerably hot, because of the surrounding sea in the cool evenings; and even on the Posillipo we could be cool when the sun went down. But NY has been pretty relentless.

[. . .]

A short piece of my novel in progress, dealing with unnamed Hong Kong in those years, appeared some weeks ago in The New Yorker. It is a portion of a subplot, but made a fairly coherent short story. When we meet I'll press a copy on you, if I may, as I'd be interested to know what you feel about such representations of oriental existence. I'm also restraining myself from asking a few more "Japanese" questions. Perhaps it will be a relief to you to hear that my characters will soon leave Japan for western lands, where their destinies will I trust be resolved.

[. . .] I'm sending this off so that written thanks at least will reach you soon. Can we know what the work will be that is to be dedicated to what—with no Japanese flourishes—we may call your unworthy but admiring friends Francis and Shirley?

CAPRI, NOVEMBER 4, 1987

Dear Donald—

A word to be in touch, give you our news, and hope you're well and that your travels were all joyful and successful. We received news from you that you were heading for the low countries too late to send word to Japan; and, not having your European address, hoped we might have a call from you while you were on your first or second trip. [. . .] We have had a somewhat disconnected and swift-moving autumn in

Italy, very hot at first; then magnificent, warm, clear, broken only by a few days of colossal storm. Today, with the Tramonta blowing, is the first day with chill in the air—air, that is, on Capri, crystalline and itself like some experience of a past time. "Keen, fitful gusts are whispering here and there" and, at evening "the stars look very cold about the sky." Yet today we lunched together—with one other table—at the Arco Naturale outdoors, I not wearing stockings (which I have scarcely put on all autumn) and with sweaters merely hung on our shoulders. The island is silent, with a good emptiness.

This reminds me that in Rome last week we went to Keats' grave, at the beautiful Cimitero Acattolico beside the pyramid of Caius Cestius. . . . a heavenly place that reconciles one to cemeteries and their implications. The corner where Keats is buried is particularly lovely. The other day a young man—probably American—came with a book (I think it was "The Waning of the Middle Ages") to sit in the sun on a bench that is placed near the grave, and told us he often comes there to read. We had spent part of the previous morning reading in the cloister of Sant'Andrea delle Fratte (that orange grove near Piazza di Spagna, unvisited by tourism). As we sat, we heard first a male voice singing an aria, somewhere nearby; then a soprano. Obviously "live", as they hesitated, sang the same phrase over, and so on. Opening a door we found a singing lesson in progress—a piano, a teacher, a beautiful Italian girl & a delicate young oriental tenor. Much inviting of us to enter, which we did on that and a subsequent occasion. Always some humane experiences of the kind in this land.

In addition to my groans over my real work, I am trying to complete that article on Naples for the Encycl. Britannica [. . .]. Fortunately, the man I deal with by phone at Chicago HQ is extremely civilised, and—although he cannot change the conditions—sympathetic to my complaints about lack of space, lack of a map (preposterous!), the quality of the preceding article on Naples—although the old one, in the great edition, was long and excellent. As "Naples" lies in the Encyc. between Napoleon and Nanking, they cannot see cutting out any of the contiguous pages—yet a proper bibliography alone should take up half the space they are allotting me.

We're thinking of going to Siena—always important to me—next week to see an exhibition of late mediaeval and Renaiss. wooden sculptures, very beautiful. Then we will be near our departure. Our neighbour's place has come on a lot, but is still beset by works eternally reinvented by our landlords. The beauty of the sea there in this season is indescribable; and we now have a full view of the Vesuvius, as we persuaded the tree surgeons at Villa Roseberry next door to do away with a sick ilex (we had out the evil eye on it previously) and some overgrown conifers that obstructed our panorama.

Now we look forward to seeing you in NY, with the hope that your "extra" visit is confirmed. [. . .] it will be good to hear how you fared on European visits, and how your trip to Venice went. Just a year ago we were there; wonderful stay, which seems a moment ago.

Good work, good things, much affection from us both—Shirley

TOKYO, NOVEMBER 7, 1987

Dear Shirley,

It seems like a very long time since I last heard from you. [. . .]

I visited Europe twice in September-October. It was rather exhausting, especially the flight from Paris to Tokyo last week, from which I am only now recovering. But it was worth it! The first occasion was a gathering of orientalists from France and the US (with a scattering of other nationalities). The subject of the conference was the possibility of greater cooperation between European & American scholars of East Asia. I'm all in favor of cooperation, especially if it means a trip to Paris, but I still cling to the old fashioned notion of scholarship as a process effected all by oneself with as little interference (or cooperation) as possible. I am clearly in the minority.

The second journey was occasioned by a conference in Venice called "Rethinking Japan". I'm not sure how much rethinking was done, but Venice was wonderful and the other people were extremely agreeable. Best of all was my first opera at La Fenice, <u>Beatrice di Tenda</u> by Bellini. I had never previously seen the opera though I have Sutherland's recording. The theatre is exquisite, & the performance was worthy. We were all invited to a chamber music concert held in the Scuola di San Rocco. You can easily imagine the effect of music heard in such magnificent surroundings.

Yesterday I had a telephone call that makes it seem likely I will be invited to Italy in April. My itinerary will include ten days in Naples, plus lectures in Rome, Milan, and perhaps elsewhere. It sounds ideal. The only thing that could make that month even better would be the presence of you and Francis in Italy at that time.

[. . .]

My best to you & Francis. Yours, Donald

NEW YORK, FEBRUARY 4, 1988

Dear Donald—

Thank you very much for your so welcome letter.

[. . .]

Could I bother you with a couple of Occupation (of Japan) questions again? I think I told you that I visited, in 1947, the military hospital of the Australian and British occupation troops on the island of Ita Jima near Kure. However, there was a large central American Occupation at Tokyo, I think? Could you tell me where the main American hospital (for troops and their families) was, and whether it had been a Japanese hospital previously? (On Ita Jima, the hospital had been previously the naval academy, if I'm right?) Whereabouts in Tokyo (if in Tokyo the main hospital was) would the American hospital have been? Do you remember if it was well regarded? Did it take any Japanese patients?—ie, Japanese presumably working for the US forces. (However, this last question is not important.)

In those times, we (at least) needed a pass from the US forces for travel by train. I do not remember how long the train journey from Tokyo to Kure was. Could you make an approximate guess? There were various domestic air routes, but these too were under MacArthur's control of course; and I don't remember if there was any flight between Kure and Tokyo.

My last question (I trust): What library was there in English for the Occupation forces? This I never knew anything about, but now I wonder and for my writing would like to know whether some central library was set up for the Occupation forces or whether small library services were dispersed through the sites of army headquarters. Could there have been anything good of this kind? Were Japanese libraries accessible (ie free of control) to scholars like yourself at that time?

Please forgive such troublesome questions—and please disregard if they seem too complicated. My hope is that they can be answered readily and without preliminary enquiries—ie, from your memory. The questions about travel might be a nuisance, and can be forgotten if so. These matters amount to few words in the "Japanese" chapters (three only) of my novel, yet you of all people will know how one wants to get such things right.

Buon divertimento, buon lavore, buon ritorno. We'll telephone you after the 16th in New York—with all affectionate greetings meantime from us both—Shirley

TOKYO, MARCH 23, 1988

Dear Shirley,

[. . .]

I was really very happy to see you and Francis again. Of course, I think of you both very often, but it was especially on seeing you again that I realized how important your friendship is. To think that for years I assumed that once I reached the university retiring age I would head for Japan and never return!

I have been busy, as usual. Two weeks ago there was a large scale gathering of Japanologists from many countries. The opening address was given by Claude Levi-Strauss. I was impressed by his vitality & his readiness to investigate Japanese culture, though in almost every respect it is quite different from his previous studies. Of course, he does not pretend to be an expert on Japan, but he clearly has read what is available in translation. I gave a talk later that day on Japanese literature in the world. Usually, when Japanese discuss this subject they confine themselves to lists of foreign translations of Japanese works of literature, but I tried to show that Japanese writers have always been "in the world", even if not translated, to the degree that they were receptive to & influenced by foreign literature. So much attention has been given of late to the seeming recrudescence of Japanese nationalism, but the cosmopolitanism of the Japanese, who for many centuries accepted a rather humble place within the orbit of Chinese civilization, and during the past century, of western civilization, is either ignored or derided as "imitation". I took the occasion to express my growing disenchantment with Lafcadio Hearn. Hearn is not taken seriously in the West any longer, but in Japan he is revered. He is known by the Japanese name he adopted, & there is even a Shinto shrine in his honor, meaning that he has been accepted into the pantheon of Japanese gods. I approve of this example of cosmopolitanism, but not of his insistence on how much better the Japanese were before the blight of western civilization affected them. I'm more and more convinced that "rootless cosmopolitanism" (so often attacked & rarely defended) is the only way we can avoid the madness of nationalism.

I am to leave for Italy on the 4th of April. I asked for the Excelsior & they agreed! It will come out of my pocket, but that's all right— I hadn't expected to earn any money. The one unpleasant feature is the strong request of the people at the Oriental Institute of the University of Naples for two-hour lectures every day except Saturday & Sunday. Only one lecture will be for the general public (in a cinema!), but two hours a day is more teaching than I have ever done before. I suppose I can get them to lighten the load a bit, but the desire for instruction must originate in the fact that they haven't had anyone to teach Japanese literature for some years. It is flattering to think that perhaps they _really_ want me to teach them. It will be a new experience, in any case. I have been surprised too by the unusually academic nature of the lectures requested. "Research perspectives in the history of Japanese literature".

No doubt everything will be more enjoyable in practice than in prospect. The maddening slowness of mail between Japan and Italy makes negotiation impossible, but I can count on the Italians to see to it that my stay is enjoyable.

On the plane returning home from New York (and later) I read _Shirley_. At times I was carried away to the extent of thinking that this is one of the best English novels, but I kept hoping (in vain, alas) for some grand development that would make the characters come alive. The themes are absorbing, & hopelessness of women in a society where they have only one chance of happiness—a good marriage—is movingly expressed. The unrest caused by the introduction of spinning machines was so well presented as to make most novels of the period seem unconcerned with the real world. But it is hard for us to sympathize with the mill owner who mercilessly tracks down disgruntled employees, & the humor is so ponderous that one yearns for some disaster to cut short the farce! But, no doubt thanks to Japanese literature, I find myself more and more interested in women novelists of the past. I really would rather read the Brontë sisters than Dickens or Trollope etc.

All my best to you and Francis. Yours, Donald

POSTCARD, CAPRI, MAY 27, 1988

Dear Donald—

Thank you so much for your greeting—how good that you saw San Clemente & the SS Quattro Coronati; and so much else all over Italy. We only regretted seeing so little of you here. Our Bologna stay was splendid—what a magnificent city—the only big town I know that has actually got better (in civic responsibility, state of conservation, elimination of traffic, etc) in the last twenty years. Here, great beauty of weather & place. Also, two unforgettable Pollini recitals (one of chamber music, all Brahms) at the San Carlo. We're all lucky. We trust your news, of health particularly, is all good? Best affection to you from us both—Shirley

CAPRI, JUNE 16, 1988

Dear Donald,

Thank you so much for the kind letter and photographs, received today. We sat in the bar next to the funicolare (a caffè with beautiful view, of course, & particularly pleasant in these mornings when the piazza itself is abuzz and <u>troppo affollata</u>, read it, and sent you many messages by mental telex.

[. . .]

When you speak of spending half the year in Venice, does it mean that such a possibility is open to you? Well, it is a miracle of beauty and survival. I do think one might exhaust its "novelty", but only after years; and the great works would only grow more precious. It is perhaps a sense of confinement, and the lack of natural things (other than the sea) that would make me hesitate to spend long stretches of time there. But two or three months would be beautiful. Do you know, out on the Fondamenta Nuove, the Church of the Madonna dell'Orto, wonderful and filled with great pictures? It was restored by English friends-of-Venice, the money being raised and the work being directed by John Pope-Hennessy. A few paces from it, a lovely old palazzo has been made into a charming and authentic hotel, the hotel Madonna dell'Orto. At the rear of the hotel there is a true garden, large for Venice and with splendid trees. It is far from the heart of the city, and that wd perhaps be troublesome for a short stay. But we're always thinking we might go for, say, three weeks, spending the first week in nearer San Marco and the balance of the stay out in that extremely interesting part of Venice—a short walk, after all, by Capri standards, from the more familiar sites, and a walk that passes through delightful scenes such as Campo dei Mori. [. . .]

Here, much to say—but it can be summed up in the word beautiful, too. The month of June has been divine in weather and in the peacefulness of Capri. Only on Saturdays and Sundays does hell break loose, and even then all go to the sea and leave us alone until evening.

You don't speak of your health, and we hope we can assume from that that all is well? We do hope so, and that work and life itself are full and pleasurable. With all affection from us both—Shirley

TOKYO, JULY 6, 1988

Dear Shirley,

It is always a delight to find a letter from you in my mailbox, but when opening it is preceded by a flourish of trumpets—in this case the magnificent stamps showing the Teatro S. Carlo and the Piazza Giuseppe Verdi in Salerno—it really becomes a special occasion. I haven't collected stamps since I was 17, but I still feel the allure.

[...]

I have not heard anything from the University of Venice about the suggestion that was made in April by one of the professors that I spend a protracted period there. At that moment, walking in the quiet of the streets that were lit not by neon but by discreetly placed lanterns here and there, I was ready to spend the rest of my life in Venice. I may still (if invited) wish to spend some months there, but at the moment the one thing I want to do most is to complete my history of Japanese literature. It goes so slowly. Reading an eleventh-century text with annotations of the unhelpful kind—not revealing the meaning of a passage but, say, the source of a borrowed quotation—I often have the feeling of working at my very limit. But it also gives me great pleasure, as you can imagine.

I have almost a drawer full of picture postcards of Italy. I owe so many marvelous places to you. I must have written you of my walk from the Excelsior to Santa Maria del Carmine. The walk itself, along the coast, was more frightening (cars parked in such a way that one could not walk on the pavement but had to take one's chances in the road) than enjoyable, but it made the arrival even more exciting. What a wonderful church! Later, I bought some picture postcards dealing with Masaniello's revolt that show the church in the background. I am trying sporadically to learn some Italian vocabulary from opera libretti. Of course, I knew already all the words for revenge, daggers, ardent love, contemptible monsters and other typical elements in opera, but I now can say "to grumble" (brontolare) and "to make fun of" (corbellare), both from the first scene of that enchanting opera of Rossini, <u>Il Viaggio a Reims</u>, which was only recently discovered. There is no telling when I will either want to grumble or make fun of some one, so I shall treasure these new acquisitions.

I hope that all goes well with your work. My best to you and Francis, as always.

Yours, Donald

Did I write that I read Edel's biography of Henry James? I was most impressed. It is really a biography, though many biographies of late have tended to be novels.

POSTCARD, NEW YORK, AUGUST 21, 1988

Dear Donald,

A word in haste, having got your card yesterday—thank you for your message and your concern; and I'm a bit aghast that you obviously haven't received a letter I sent from Italy at least six weeks ago, before we left Naples to visit friends at Fano on the Adriatic (from Fano, then, to Rome and NY). Perhaps it will arrive—the Neapolitan post takes the summer off, we find. But I'm mortified that you had no word. Yes we are both sunk in work at present which is a good way of sinking no doubt. The heat in the city was infernal from the time of our return—really remarkable, and (almost) interesting in its cruel portentousness. Only the last two or three days has the incubus lifted which had never altered, day or night and unprecedented.

I'm glad to think you, too, have a volcano—a smoking one, at that. [...]

We return to Italy soon after Labour Day. All our affectionate greetings, and our "auguri" for your work—Shirley

TOKYO, AUGUST 30, 1988

Dear Shirley,

I was much relieved to receive your letter with the interesting enclosures. No, I had not received your previous letter. It is strange how
one tends to trust the postal systems of the different countries,
despite all evidence. One assumes that after one has dutifully placed a
stamp on the envelope and then pushed the letter into the designated
receptacle, it will then without fail reach its destination. Perhaps that
was even true at some time in the golden age of the Postal Service.
But again and again I have had the experience of <u>knowing</u> that a letter had been sent to me yet never receiving it. Nevertheless, my faith
is abiding, and so each time I have evidence that still another letter
has found its way into the yawning maw of the Dead Letter Office,
I feel the transience of the world anew. And, as the Japanese used to
say, my sleeve is wet with tears.

You mentioned in your letter, the one I received I mean, that you
would be in New York until after Labor Day. I blush to admit it, but
I don't know when that is. The reason why I am interested in this
fact of American history is that the book which I have dedicated to
you and Francis will be ready about the middle of September. There
is obviously no hurry about delivering a book that deals mainly with
events of nine hundred years ago, but I would like to be able to tell the
Columbia University Press where to send the book. If you will be in
New York until a certain date, they might send a copy by special mes-
senger in order to foil the evil designs of the local post offices. [. . .]

There is a possibility I may teach at the University of Rome in
November of next year. There is some sort of exchange agreement
between that university and Columbia, and they asked if I could lecture there for about three weeks. I believe I told you that I gave two
lectures there, each of an hour and a half in the space of three and a
half hours!

At the moment I'm going over the copyedited manuscript of my book on Japanese diaries.[1] It is to be published in New York by Holt, who published the volumes of my history. I have been most discouraged and upset by the remarks of the copyeditor. She knows nothing about Japan, as she cheerfully admits, and her queries (as one of the ignorant public) are sometimes to the point. But I have the impression that she does not understand what I have been trying to do. I have used the diaries to find Japanese people of the past who can still speak to us. For my purposes it does not matter much if a particular diary is well or badly written, as long as there is something in it which inspires me to comment on it, to find something of lasting significance in it. But the copyeditor seizes upon every indication that I honestly make that a diary is not a literary masterpiece to urge that I delete it. And anything that seems less than a true diary by her standards is also fated for the block. I shall resist, and no doubt in the end there will be some kind of compromise, but it is an unpleasant beginning to the process of producing a book.

Another problem arises from her fears that if ever I mentioned that a work is notably masculine or feminine in style I am sternly warned that this will open me to charges of sexism. It doesn't matter that I may be praising women's writings, or saying that the diaries by men are not as well written; if I dare to mention the words masculine or feminine I am likely to be viciously attacked. At the moment I think I would prefer to be attacked, rather than change what seems to me to be a legitimate way of treating the materials, but no doubt the publisher fears bombs.

After reading your last letter (some months ago) I decided I really must read Dickens again, and I have at last implemented this decision by reading <u>Hard Times</u>. I think I like it better than any previous Dickens novel I have read. I always have trouble with his drollery and the names of the characters, but in this instance the work is so solidly made that my objections are swept away.

As ever, Donald

CAPRI, OCTOBER 17, 1988

Dear Donald—

Please forgive this unexpected stationary—from the beautiful hotel near Positano where we've just spent a few days, in the course of attending the wedding of the Knights'[2] daughter—a most delightful affair, so Italian in the best and ultimate sense, a synthesis of perfect simplicity, easy amplitude, much beauty, laughter, high spirits, and just the right tinge of solemnity. The peak of the celebration was an Epithalamium, unexpected even by Ella, delivered by Carlo[3] without notes—he had composed this charming poem in the preceding days and since it was by no means short, put me in mind of Metastasio by reciting it in high spirit over several minutes. The beautiful hot day, the coast in splendour, a riot of flowers around us as we all sat at lunch at the San Pietro . . . Well, by now you may even feel you know too much about the event.

The occasion was almost too much for us, coming immediately on the receipt of your wonderful book with its dedication which moves us both and makes us proud and happy. The book was brought to us from the gatehouse at our Posillipo place by the driver who had come to take us to Positano for the wedding. We debated whether to bring it with us but decided it would get tossed about in the luggage and be boxed about the ears. Now we think we must have been mad, as we both long to have it in our hands and to read it—not to mention reading over the dedication a good few times. Well, Francis says that on this occasion he feels the justice of his father's perpetual question (whenever Francis had any notice in the press), "What have you done to deserve this honour?" And honour, we feel, in the true sense—friendship is the best honour one can have; and the linking of one's best feelings to a fine work touches heart and mind. Thank you, dear Donald, from both of us and from the heart. When we're all together again in NYC we'll hope to "festeggiare" this volume and all its associations for us. The book came with a kind letter from Jennifer Crewe (surely an English name?) at Columbia UP, and we're writing to thank her. It took over three weeks by air. As to your letters, and ours, I won't bore you with their adventures in the post—although I wonder if my July letter has any chance of ever turning up. I do find a complete disappearance of a letter very unusual, although it's happened to me once or twice before. However, the summer mails in Italy are extremely strange, and one hears of disgruntled postini who tip their complement of letters into a rubbish dump, etc. (At the UN, a filing clerk—not myself—for years threw out all the correspondence he was supposed to file; no one noticed it, and he was only caught by indiscreetly confiding his "method" to a colleague.)

[. . .]

Italian institutions are the devil, in making proposals and then falling silent. However, the "convegno" which we were invited to in Bologna last April—which was the stimulus for a splendid Emilian stay—has crazily given rise to invitations to "Professoressa" Hazzard to "speak" throughout this sometimes deluded nation—not only deluded in the English sense, but to be "delusa" in the Italian sense if I took up these rash suggestions. I did give a short talk at a rather marvellous gathering at Villa Pignatelli here last week (where you and I saw an exhibition of 17th century painters once): it was a memorial "convegno" for Roberto Pane, and extremely moving—first of all for the almost incredible diversity of themes, all of which he had mastered; and then because some of his "enemies" (nearly every Neapolitan in a prominent scholarly or cultural position today was, if he or she is of any stature, a university pupil of Pane's; he then admonished them for having, as he considered it, joined the hated establishment by becoming museum directors, etc) made moving speeches about him. There were of course also many who had managed to stay on good terms with this formidable man; and those who loved him included ourselves. A Florentine professor made a wonderful talk that brought Pane vividly alive, with his outrageous and inspired decrees and his fearless pronouncements. (Of a modern architect whose work—familiar to New Yorkers, of expensive honey-combed apartment buildings and high rises—was hailed as genius, Pane said "Yes, it takes genius to reconstruct the 'bassi' on the top floor". The "bassi" being those cubicles in which thousands of Nea-politans live right on the street, for instance in Spaccanápoli. Pane was also quoted against specialisation—e.g., the exhaustive concen-tration on a single painter's work, and so on—as having remarked that such specialisation was more evocative of a trained dog than of a fulfilled human being.) When asked to speak, I had said that I would like to be among the series of brief speakers (no more than quarter-hour each). I kept my bargain, but most of the others ran on, disregarding even the little alarm bell that rang when they had exag-gerated unconscionably. Italians do love these speaking marathons, nightmarish to us. But the Pane congress was quite exceptional, and often brilliant. He clearly made it animate with his presence and his "risata sogghignante"; and at times one felt his thunderbolt might fall—as when the mayor (of Naples) exploited the opportunity to speak of the wonderful "developments" now hideously proposed for the ancient centre. However, the next speakers pulverised this theme. (Which nevertheless remains a ghastly threat here. The ancient cen-tre is the last nucleus in mid-Naples for the speculators to make their billions, and we have learned now that every wildest fantasy of "urban development" can be realised if there is enough money in it and no official morality whatever. If there is any posterity, I should think the Koch-Trump era in New York City may be looked back upon as a threshold to the new stage of ruthless real estate exploitation we now seem burdened with forever.)

Forgive this rambling. Other events, Napoli '99 "convegno" on the Emperor Frederick III, culminating in the "unveiling" of the restored arch of renaissance sculptures at the Castel Nuovo. This was really marvellous, done with great taste in an evening ceremony, to which Cossiga (pres. of Italy) came, but—as is often the case with the Italian president—said nothing, not even a word. This obviously has its advantages in a president, but the tradition does make him seem more of an icon than ever, although not a particularly attractive one. We spent a few days in Rome, clambering about an excavation under a beloved church and discovering extraordinary things in a peripheral connection to Galiani. [. . .] Now, much work to do, and new experiences no doubt. Among the deluded invitations to me to "speak", God help us, is a tempting offer to bring me from New York to Florence in January, for another "convegno" at the Univ. of Florence. But when would I ever work if I did not stay put in NYC for the winter, especially as I now must finish my novel? Besides, I really have no more "speeches" left in me, and hope never to "speak" again. The speaking of "our" presidential candidates is dismaying, isn't it?—We will register our absentee votes for Dukakis, and be "pleased" if by a miracle the Democrats shd win. But the level is shameful, the populace in general appallingly intent on having leaders of this low calibre, and meantime the initiative in world change passes "suddenly" to the Soviets, whose efforts to break out of their monolithic bondage provide the modern adult political interest (despite the anguish of the NY Times at the prospect that anything might conceivably improve in Russia).

[. . .] I wonder whether, in Japan, you escape Christmas? Christmas has a habit of finding one out in any refuge—as I remember from Christmases spent in eg Morocco, where Joyeux Noël could not be dodged. You speak of Dickens, and a few years ago I bravely did read "A Christmas Carol" at its very season, to find halfway through that my sleeve actually was wet with tears. Yes, as you say, he is outrageous—but doesn't his genius consist in that? David Copperfield, Our Mutual Friend, Tale Of Two Cities, and above all Great Expectations seemed to me superhuman—and yet of course intensely human: wonderful. Hard Times has particular appeals for me. Oh, Mr Gradgrind! What presence, what courage. The names, as you say, are incorrigible—yet with this aspect of Dickens, as with names in Patrick White too, life seems to catch up. Some names are in real life staggeringly appropriate—and there is in fact a phenomenon called <u>nomen et omen</u> (de Gaulle, for instance, or Rupert Murdstone-Murdoch).

[. . .]

Yes, Edel has fulfilled himself with his work on James. I think he has also matured in many ways in his writing of the work, and that his other recent books—eg on Bloomsbury—have not been sufficiently appreciated. There is an academic prejudice against him—and, I suspect, a rage that he "took hold" of James nearly forty years ago, when few others were interested in understanding James at such length, and has presided over "the field" ever since, without coming through the usual academic strongholds, without the approval of Trilling etc, and with a fresh, non-unctuous attitude of his own. (For my part, a bit less reverence in the earlier vols would have been welcome, for I think some difficult and unpalatable aspects of James were soft-pedalled, and perhaps he has been exalted somewhat beyond his due; although I know that this opinion is a heresy at present.)

Francis thanks you most warmly for the Maxim Ducamp post-card. How perfectly that Mutt-and-Jeff pair of Maxim and Gustave were contrasted on their Egyptian journey—the journalist versus the artist; and how their writings faithfully portray that.

I look forward to your operatic Italian. Myself, I was first drawn to the Italian language through the poetry of Leopardi; and subsequently, through a multitude of other poets, treasured up a sense of Italian that remains the centre of my feeling for the language. Yet I confessed that a time came when a memorising of irregular verbs, a grappling with the terrible subjunctives, etc, dawned as an inevitable task, an entry fee to "communication" not to mention conversation.

To you, all that will seem child's play after mastering Japanese. But it does go on forever . . .

Francis says, To think that Donald has been present in Japan throughout the "calvario" (calvario, though, is perhaps not a Shinto concept)—the capezzale, literally and correctly—of the Emperor. This imperial figure has been with us so long, it will be a parting from one's experience. I don't remember a time when he wasn't there, and yet always unreal and almost invisible. Even Australian cartoonists during the war didn't know quite what to do with Hirohito as an arch enemy; and had to settle for Tojo, whose teeth were infinitely magnified and whose eyes were intensely slitted in those days of unselfconscious racism. (Now we have self-conscious racism, I hardly know which to "prefer".) In my childhood we had "elders" who were apparently immortal—Shaw, Einstein, Wells, Bertrand Russell, Churchill, Smuts, Ghandi, Beecham . . . It seemed these wd see us through our lifetimes. Well, Hirohito, unobtrusively, has just about managed it.

[. . .]

With our most affectionate & grateful appreciation of your truly named "Pleasures of Japanese Literature" and its precious dedication— with friendliest <u>auguri</u> from us both—Shirley

TOKYO, NOVEMBER 22, 1988

Dear Shirley and Francis,

Thank you so much for your letters. I believe that this is the first time I have ever fallen so far behind in responding, but I think you will agree, when you hear the gory details, that there has been cause. For reasons which I cannot possibly explain I have been faced with the prospect of delivering four lectures on completely unrelated topics within a period of six days. The first of them went off well today, so

I feel I can allow myself the pleasure of writing you, rather than confronting "women in Japanese literature" or "Japanese impressions of European art in the 1870s."

First of all, I am delighted that you like the book I dedicated to you. It fortunately does not look like a university press book; in fact, it is the most attractive book I have ever published. I wrote a somewhat similar book in 1953, while I was still at Cambridge. I hope that I have learned something about Japanese literature during the past 35 years! To my astonishment, that book, long since out of print in England, is still fulfilling its original function of introducing Japanese literature to people who know nothing about it. Earlier this year a translation into modern Greek appeared, and I have signed a contract for a Romanian translation. Japan has been slow in reaching the Balkans.

[. . .]

I have read "The Abbé Galiani" with much pleasure. After reading it I looked him up in the Encyclopaedia Britannica to see if he appeared. He does (or did, they keep dropping people), but in the two paragraphs they devote to the man they suggest nothing of the interest in Francis's article. I look forward to reading the book.

I am approaching the end of my long stay in Japan. It should come as no surprise to me, but I have not accomplished nearly as much as I had hoped. The lectures all over the place were one cause. Reading the old literature was also more time-consuming than I had anticipated. And there were the weeks spent with the manuscript of the diary book. But I have made progress, and for that I am grateful. I shall be returning to New York on January 12th.

[. . .]

After a summer that consisted entirely of rain, followed by a September that was more of the same, we have had wonderful weather. I have even bought a humidifier—unheard of in Japan, where the humidity is rarely omitted from conversations. It is getting cold. I hope it will get very cold, so that my return to New York will be painless. But even if the[re are] icy gales awaiting me at Kennedy Airport I know that we shall have a warm reunion.

As ever, Donald

TOKYO, AUGUST 4, 1989

Dear Shirley,

It seems an eternity since I last heard from you. I hope that this silence means that you and Francis have been too busy with your books to write, but I fear that it means no more than that another letter has been destroyed at the post office by some new machine. I once received a letter which had been torn open by one machine and sealed again by another. In the process, the original letter was augmented by a sheaf of Sears Roebuck receipts destined for someone in New Jersey. [. . .]

I have been working hard on my history of Japanese literature. It is a good feeling to feel each day that I have added something to the manuscript, though I fear I may be getting rather garrulous in the excitement of being able to devote myself mainly to my work and not to writing trivial articles or delivering one more speech on Japan in the World. I am working now on early 13th century poetry. I have decided to try to translate the poems into the original forms, though I can't manage anything like the original rhythms. Sometimes the English language seems resolved not to let me get away with this experiment, but after much coaxing I can generally come up with the line in seven syllables. I made a great discovery a few weeks ago. Many English nursery rhymes open with lines in seven syllables, though this is not usual in other poetry. Jack and Jill went up the hill. Jack be nimble, Jack be quick. Mary had a little lamb. I am not sure precisely what this proves.

This has been an eventful summer. There was a fairly serious earthquake with its epicentre in the town on the coast where I have a little place. I suffered no damage, but some people lost almost of their chinaware. Worst of all, it has been ascertained that a new volcano has just been born in the sea, and people are freely predicting that it or another volcano will soon erupt nearby. All this reminds me of the letter of Pliny about Pompeii which you kindly copied for me. What a way to go! Somehow I can't take volcanoes as seriously as wars. I was not actually there when the earthquake took place, but I was there the previous night when there were smaller but disquieting shocks. We have also had the usual typhoons. It is really perplexing why the Japanese are so pleased with their climate.

The English version of the book on Japanese Diaries for which I received a prize here appeared in July. I naturally asked that a copy be sent to you and Francis. [. . .]

I hope that New York is not as torrid as last year. This is the height of the summer heat, but I rather like it, at least in comparison to the torrential rains we had last week. I have not seen such rains since Bombay.

When will your article on Waldheim appear?[4] Perhaps it has already appeared but I almost never see the New Yorker when I am in Japan.

Please send a postcard when you have a moment.

Yours Donald

TOKYO, OCTOBER 23, 1989

Dear Shirley,

I was very glad to have your letter from New York, written just before your departure for Italy, and today I received the copy of the article which had appeared in Newsweek. I had in fact seen that article earlier. Someone in California whom I have never heard of before sent the article along with xerox copies of several Japanese documents he found in a foxhole somewhere in the Pacific during the war. In return for his great kindness in sending me the Newsweek article he wanted a complete translation of the Japanese documents. (They were a complete record of a motor pool, giving precise data on exactly when cars were borrowed and returned, and a savings bank passbook.) I am afraid that the age of the disinterested friendly gesture may be coming to an end!

[. . .]

I leave, as I have just said, on the 13th of November for Rome. I will take another plane for Milan a few hours after my arrival, and will stay in Milan with friends until the 20th of November when I go to Rome. The accommodations in Rome are not available until that day. I am not sure whether I shall be in Milan for the whole week. I really would like to go to Mantua at a time of day when the palace is open, and my friend Soichi Furuta is now staying at a castle owned by Mary de Rachewiltz, the daughter of Ezra Pound, and has invited me to the castle in Merano. There is also a faint possibility I may be asked to give a lecture at the University of Bologna.

I am not really sure what is expected of me in Rome. I have been asked to give three lectures on subjects that are familiar to me, so I do not anticipate too much work. I should be able to visit you at a time that is convenient to you. I hope that there will be such a time, but I know how busy you are with your work.

[. . .]

My firm resolve to learn Italian this summer crumbled in the face of reality. I listened to the tapes one day. I had no trouble saying all the things the tapes ordered me to say, but I surely have forgotten them all by now.

[. . .]

All my best to you and Francis,
As ever, Donald.

NEW YORK, APRIL 16, 1990

Dear Shirley,

I have meant to write you ever since reading the piece in the New York Times book review by Anatole Broyard. I had always supposed he was a heartless monster whose only pleasure consisted in sneering at defenseless authors. His review of my <u>Dawn to the West</u> opened with something like "This book is like an endless nightmare." But lo! He has a heart, after all. Or perhaps he has been taught humility by being stricken in the manner he describes. In any case, it gave me great pleasure to read how much your book had meant to him as he lay in a hospital bed, fearful of death. He probably would have appreciated it just as much even under normal circumstances, but his pride might have kept him from saying so.

[. . .]

The Columbia spring term is almost over. It went by very quickly. I have made good progress on the final volume of my history of Japanese literature and, for the first time, feel I shall complete it in the foreseeable future. I may be too optimistic, but it is a pleasant sensation. At times I have thought the task Sisyphean, each chapter completed suggesting a new chapter I hadn't planned on writing.

I am looking forward to my forthcoming Italian journey. How strange that it all began with my sudden impulse to visit you in Capri—was it five years ago? And every year since then I have managed to return. This time I really won't have to <u>do</u> anything except look solemn as the chairman of a meeting. If the stars are favorable, there may be an opera at La Fenice. The terrible <u>Falstaff</u> I saw in Rome last December hasn't changed my desire to see operas in their native habitat.

All my best to you and Francis.
Yours, Donald

TOKYO, JULY 16, 1990

Dear Shirley,

[. . .]

Thank you for your letter with the usual grand display of Italian postage stamps. The Japanese also print beautiful stamps, but they tend to be available for one day only at the local post office. Perhaps you have a man at the post office in Capri who puts aside beautiful stamps for you. Or, more likely, you are more provident than I and do not miss opportunities to buy the stamps.

Today is the first really hot day of summer. We have been having rather chilly rain and I was romanticizing about the glory of bright summer afternoons—but not this! It certainly must have been just as hot in the past as it is now, but I survived without air conditioning somehow. For about ten years I used to spend my summers in Japan, teaching the rest of the year, and I chose to spend them in Kyoto, the hottest place in the whole country. I evidently have become much less resilient than I once was.

I am slowly but (I think) surely proceeding with my history. One alarming feature: the chapters keep getting longer and longer, even though the works of literature discussed are not necessarily as good as those in the earlier chapters. In fact, it is probably the case that the better the work the less I have said about it, if only because the best works are available in English translation, and the temptation is to say to the reader: Go read it for yourself. Second-rate books are also more likely to be of interest to the student of cultural history than the masterpieces, which stand in solitary grandeur, aloof from their times.

[. . .]

I am always rather embarrassed to mention any honor I receive in Japan because I do not know how seriously it should be taken— whether I received it for my solid scholarship or just because the

Japanese, as a gesture towards internationalism, want to honor some foreigner, and they have chosen me because of my hoary locks. Anyway, I was surprised and very pleased to learn that I had been elected to the Japan Academy as an honorary (that is, foreign) member. I keep asking myself, "Do they really mean _me_?" The Japanese members of the Academy receive a fairly substantial annual grant and (I think) can ride on the trains free of charge, but I doubt this applies to foreigners as well. I imagine that I must be the only foreign member (I think there are 20 in all) who actually lives in Japan, at least part of the year.

Today I leave for the island of Shikoku. It is famous for its 88 temples which pilgrims visit in succession in the hopes of securing relief from sickness and so on. The national television network has divided the temples among some twenty-five or thirty people, and has scheduled live television broadcasts of these people visiting the temples and making appropriate comments. I have been given three temples in a pleasant part of the island. I have been sent the videotapes of two previous broadcasts. The level of the comments is not unusually high. As the visitor approaches the temple he sees the great gate and comments, "Splendid gate!" A bit farther on is a pond, to which the visitor responds, "How clear the water is!" Still farther on is the main temple building, which elicits, "Simple but powerful architecture!" The inside of the temple draws forth a similar comment, "The product of simple faith!" And so on. Now that I know what is expected of me, I shall of course follow tradition.

I shall be back in New York very briefly in October for a festive dinner in honor of a Japanese financier who gave a million dollars a couple of years ago to Colombia. I do not look forward to the long journey for such an occasion, but it would be wonderful if I could see you and Francis again. My best wishes to you both.

Yours, Donald

I forgot to congratulate Francis on the completion of his book. I look forward to reading it.

TOKYO, SEPTEMBER 23, 1990

Dear Shirley,

[. . .]

The summer in Japan was the hottest I have ever experienced here. It broke all kinds of records. That is a consolation, but not enough to justify the experience. As of yesterday it has become considerably cooler and—who knows?—the summer may even have ended. Despite the heat, I was able to get quite a lot of work done. Or it may be that <u>because</u> of the heat I was kept indoors and away from exhibitions of art, Kabuki and the rest. I am now working on the last chapter of my history, begun over twenty-five years ago. No, that is not quite accurate. It is the last substantive chapter, but I shall have to write a long introductory chapter in which I expose the fruits of all that I have studied during these twenty-five years. Probably I shall not finish it until the spring, in New York. I fear that there will not be a display of fireworks over the Hudson River, but I shall be content if I can celebrate with a few friends.

I shall be going to Germany on the 1st of October. An important Japanese publisher has established a prize for the translation of modern Japanese literature into foreign languages, and it will be officially announced in Frankfurt at the book fair. This is the Japan Year. I shall go to Finland for a lecture there and then on to New York for three days. It is idiotic, but I made an engagement to give a lecture in Tokyo a year ago, not knowing I would be going to Europe and America, and the people here say that it is absolutely impossible to change the date, so I must rush back.

[. . .]

All my best to you and Francis.
Yours as ever, Donald

NAPLES, OCTOBER 16, 1990

Dear Donald—

How many letters you've had from me beginning with apologies for delay in putting pen to paper—and here's another, in the eternal context of being overwhelmed by events and interruptions, and always trying to establish a working pattern that will hold firm against all intervention . . . No chance, I feel, of that. But work does get done, even so, and many pleasant things occur that make us feel lucky in this <u>manicomio</u> of a world. The present "crisis" seems to me the most foreseeable and avoidable of all of them, since the onset of the Viet Nam war. No one seems to have appetite for fighting and dying over the price of petrol—and the American public isn't yet able to discuss such matters in a context detached from hypocrisy and moral righteousness—thus, a sort of mental <u>impasse</u>.

More pleasing, and more enduring, is the great achievement of your nearly completed History—an event that recreates faith in the singular capacity to bring a mighty enterprise to its conclusion. We both do congratulate you from the heart. It is wonderful to think of, and gives a sort of elevated happiness to your friends. When we're all together again in NYC, we must have a celebration of private kind—I'm sure there will be numerous celebrations of more public sort. I wd like to read the whole now, right through—to understand it as a continuity. You must be—what?—well, excited, I should imagine?

[. . .]

The Neapolitan autumn, always beautiful, is surpassing itself this year, and for some time we've been dining outdoors. Still in summer clothes. Here, as you know, each day is an adventure, and those of October 1990 have so far been benign and spectacular—speaking personally. "Publicly", the deaths of Moravia and Patrick White were somehow shocking, although not at all unexpected. We knew both of them—both difficult men, and both, I'd say, writers who had lost impetus in later years. But, in part because of formidability, they were the kind who don't die, don't appear subject to death. The newspaper La Repubblica had, for its main headline "Senza Moravia" and it's true that he's been a presence for most Italians as long as they can remember & that the nation feels somewhat different without him. Graham Greene is also extremely ill—we called him in Antibes on his birthday (a day we'd often spent together on Capri) and he sounded very weak (although livening up as he worked up some antagonism . . .). He wrote us that he is living from transfusions. I don't know how long that can go on.

Italy is really rather alarming—order, never a great feature of this region, in some places seems to be breaking down into utter corruption and banditry. Today's news is that Gava, an arch Camorrista who has for some time been minister for the interior in the national govt, is resigning from "ill health". I dare say he won't resign his sinister activities, but at least they'll be without portfolio.

[. . .]

So—Francis' "Galiani" is done; your history is nearly done. I must get back to my pages and have something to show. With much affection, dear Donald, from us both, and with warmest congratulations and <u>auguri</u>—Shirley

CAPRI, SEPTEMBER 2, 1991

Dear Donald—

[. . .] Please forgive such a silence. We have been engulfed—but then all our friends are engulfed, and engulfment thus holds no water (if that's a permissible figure of speech . . .). When we returned to NYC and found yr letter, I had much in my mind to exchange with you.

Now we are about to leave again, in a couple of days, for Italy, and so many events and moments have poured over us all that I hardly know how to be coherent. One morning a couple of weeks ago we woke up to torrential rain—the side of a hurricane—and the news that Gorbachev had been detained, the populace had risen, and other unbelievable truths. I've been thinking of Alexander Herzen, in Rome in 1848, writing: "It's either the Second Coming or the Last Judgement". Something fine was the spectacle of the Russian people, who have remained cowed through three generations of persecutions, and, in the last quarter-century, through the expulsion and intimidation of the most gifted and courageous of their fellow citizens, now taking to the streets, climbing on the tanks, haranguing their oppressors—and standing in crowds outside the KGB palace and laughing. Well—we need not say that much trouble lies ahead, and so on. Because there is always trouble; but we are unused to the luxury of positive and unequivocal actions on the part of the public. Truth is great and shall prevail; but how long before it does, and how many uncounted lives are consumed in the great unravelling.

When we're reunited, and when the triumph of your final volume of the history is consummated, we must have a pow-wow about Dickens. What an extraordinary genius, even among genii; what a weird but profoundly sane man (Shakespeare is saner—and greater—still; but he too had a mighty grasp of weirdness); what boldness, what terrible lapses, what astonishing effect, what wisdom . . . And then, the gripping and almost visual passages—like the opening of Our Mutual Friend, or like Steerforth waving his cap. There are long stretches of filling-in, and the girls are—with few exceptions—hopelessly unreal; but one is never sorry to have read everything, every word. That central failing that the main characters are sometimes less believable than the peripheral ones, as you say, seems true for various of the Victorian novelists; perhaps because of their feeling that "virtue" (which, embodied, becomes implausible and a bore) shd be represented almost unflawed. (Daniel Deronda seems a particular example of that: Deronda himself is a mere wooden figure, while the villain, Grandcourt, is marvellously drawn. But George Eliot could be good in representing virtue in women, at least at times.) On the other hand, Pip in Great Ex, and David Copperfield are well done, even if David C has his unbelievable moments.

[. . .]

Part of our own lack of time has been, of course, work—but, in F's case, the double task of correcting 18th century book's proofs for late October publication, while at the same time completing a 1,000 page typescript of the Flaubert-George Sand correspondence. This last has now, apart from introduction, gone to the publisher. All that has made a long division in my own work and state of mind for work; and all I want, now, is to get to my own pages. Against the odds, I finished a long chapter of my novel about three weeks ago, and feel that it will now truly move on to completion if I can fight off distractions and stick to it ruthlessly. How ruthless one does have to be to get anything done—ruthless also with oneself, as Leonard Woolf pointed out. I've just read a huge life of Patrick White, by an Australian writer. Knopf will publish it next year. It's assiduous and in many ways commendable; but the life is dismaying, the compulsive cruelty and offensiveness, always combined with larger qualities. It is much worse than I imagined, although one had some sense of the long dichotomy. The later work shows disintegration, to my mind. Curious story, and utterly un-American.

This brings auguri from us both. [. . .] We must seize the day; which includes our next get-together. I hope that Italy has reverted to beautiful stamps, after those horrors of last spring. If I find good examples, I'll make them an excuse for a next bulletin. With all our best greetings ever, dear Donald, and with warm affection and congratulations from us both—Shirley

TOKYO, DECEMBER 6, 1991

Dear Shirley,

When I received your letter in September I decided to give you breathing space before I answered. I know how it feels when, having at last written a letter to a friend, one has hardly sent it off than another letter arrives. But waiting three months has been rather too discreet!

My time in Japan has been going by quickly. After completing my history of Japanese literature I felt a considerable let-down, but before long I set to work putting into English the second volume of Japanese diaries. That accomplished, I turned to translating some plays by a friend. The book, when completed, will consist of three plays and I have now translated two and a half.[5] The last play is written largely in a dialect that I don't really know, though it is not hard to find someone to help me. The problem is whether or not to try to reproduce in English something of the contrast between dialect and standard speech. Even if I could write some dialect of English (I can't) the associations would be wrong. At first the "you-all" would be transported to the Deep South, and not of Japan! There is another problem in the form of the stiff, rather unnatural language of police depositions. I really should be able to translate the play into three varieties of English, but I am afraid that is beyond my capability.

I spent three weeks in China during September. I gave a series of lectures in Japanese at the University of Hangzhou. It delighted me to think of teaching Japanese literature to Chinese, who traditionally have denied that such a thing existed. Everyone was most agreeable, and after my last lecture I was presented with a document bound in crimson velvet that proclaimed that I had been named Professor Emeritus of Hangzhou University! The city of Hangzhou is the most attractive I have seen in China, made so by a large lake on which boats silently pass. There is no shortage of ugly buildings too, some of them intruding on the view of the lake, but one can position oneself in such a way that they are blocked from sight.

I had not quite realized the extent of the destruction—brought about by the Cultural Revolution—until I visited the temples in the region. In most cases, every single object inside the buildings was destroyed, even innocuous stone tablets on which poems had been inscribed. Some of the Buddhist statues have been replaced in recent years, in part for Chinese who wish to worship them, but mainly for the tourist industry, I suppose. These new works of art are, without exception, hideous. For a very long time the reputation of the Japanese was that of imitators of China or the West, and they were often scorned for that reason; but on looking at the statues in Chinese temples and remembering the ones I have seen in Japan, how I wish that the Chinese had been able to imitate the Japanese!

Economic conditions in Hangzhou seem vastly better than those that prevailed ten years ago when I visited China. The shops are full of (extremely ugly) merchandise, and the big Friendship shops, where formerly only people furnished with foreign currency could shop, are now open to everyone. The catch is that there are two systems of prices, one for the Chinese, the other for foreigners. The Chinese government is obviously trying to keep the prices paid by Chinese down by squeezing what it can from visitors. My hotel room in Hangzhou cost more for one night (without meals) than professors receive in salary for a whole month. The salaries paid professors are in any case inadequate to live on, but they are able to augment their salaries by serving as tourist guides, etc. But, all in all, I think things have greatly improved and (at least in the big cities) the standard of living is tolerable.

I expect to return to New York on the 13th of January. Early in March there is to be a joyful celebration at Columbia of my forthcoming retirement. [. . .] I hope you will be in New York in January and that I shall have the pleasure of seeing you then.

All my warmest good wishes.
Yours, Donald

NEW YORK, SEPTEMBER 6, 1992

Dear Donald—I must first thank you from the heart for your lovely letter—which arrived, as you'll see, as more than ever an inspiriting intervention—and for the marvellous photograph enclosed, one of the best photographs I ever saw of three people having justified "transports" (not in the 18th century Australian penitential sense). We enjoyed and enjoy it, for itself and because it brings before us that unforgettable evening. Such mighty moments, where civilization becomes manifest and even in its own strange sense triumphant, are more than ever rare and precious in this weird time with its ever intensifying disintegrations around the globe. I don't write this to be apocalyptic, but because one cannot be unaware, except while working and with close friends (and of course while reading), of the palpable unease of all forms of order . . . [. . .]

I shd tell you that shortly after your letter arrived, Francis had an awful fall, which took the wind out of our collective and respective sails. Things are pretty much right again, and he escaped miraculously from worse injuries; but it took a toll, and was a bad shock to both of us. We had invited Erse Breunig's granddaughter, a lovely and intelligent girl just out of Barnard, to dinner at a little restaurant on top of Bloomingdales. (This, <u>Le Train bleu</u>, is—I suppose—a shopper's lunchtime pandemonium; but almost no one knows that it is open on Thursday evenings, when the store is open late. Quiet, one eats well, there is a fine view over the East River, etc.) We walked down Third Ave, entered the fateful portals, and got on the escalator.

As it went up Francis seemed to lose balance on left leg, and tumbled down, couldn't get up on the moving stairs, which were cutting horribly into his legs . . . "They" stopped the escalator before he was carried back to the top, a squad arrived (in terror of being sued), lifted him up, got him to a chair, when I saw that he could walk, some—at least—of the horror subsided. But it was one of those events where the abyss yawns—that abyss described in the Iliad, shortly before the encounter between Achilles and Hector that ends with Hector's death, where the fearful underworld threatens to break open, that underneath of things feared alike "by mortal and the immortal gods". I think of that passage in connection with the interior of the crater of Vesuvius . . . An ambulance was called, we found ourselves at the emergency at NY hosp, much waiting, etc. [. . .] When the gashes in F's legs were attended to, nothing seemed very wrong except contusions and shock; and we had already found a few absurdities to smile over in the institutional ongoings around us (although I shd add that everyone was helpful and a few were splendidly humane). Since then, a round of bone scans, X-rays, orthopedist, neurologist, dermatologist, therapist, endless visits to hospital and doctors' offices—that has been a large part of our lives. F only now starts to feel himself and has started a brief new work, of which more when we meet. We are hoping to go to Naples in a few days' time.

To you I will say that it has been a bit gruelling. However, we've both worked a great deal throughout, though with me that has been a struggle against a thousand daily claims on my time. One night I stayed up all through the night to get a piece of work finished, as I knew that when morning came I wd not be able to go to my desk. Francis has mercifully slept a great deal. Yesterday he seemed absolutely back to his old self, and—as I say—we have found much to laugh about even in this. Exactly ten years ago, we were recovering from his mugging at Naples—he claims that he can't be called accident-prone at ten-year intervals. A small booklet has been published of his account of the "Incident at Naples", and he says he is impatient to press a copy on you.

[. . .]

Of course we want extremely to know when your final volume of the history will come out. [. . .] Thrilling to me is the news of your "kind of autobiography". You know that we prize your brief memoirs, unique and so moving. The second book of diaries will be another revelation. And then, good lord, the biography of the Emperor Meiji. That is wonderful. I smiled over the present of a fresh fish—so practical and welcome. When I was at kindergarten, the (wonderful) Scots teacher, Miss Birrell, would round us up at Christmas, when the custom was for the little pupils to bring a giftie to the teacher, sent by one's Mamma), and tell us with gaelic frugality: "Remember, children, that you shd tell yr mothers that Miss Birrell has plenty of handker-chiefs, plenty of handkerchief sachets, plenty of quilted coat-hangers, plenty of bedsocks, plenty of slippers and lavender bags. What Miss Birrell needs is: leather gloves size seven, in dark colours; a new electric kettle; a woollen material, preferably serge, in navy blue" etc.

[. . .]

How good it is to read of your serious life, serious in the rightful true sense, with so much fine work and with pleasures of elevated kind—_ozio elevato_. I wish I could have one half of that disciplined time to write and to finish my book, which I do hope to conclude in the new year. Our lives have been—as Keats said of his own existence—like a pack of scattered cards these past few weeks. And it's done me good to re-read your letter and send at last my reply, which I needed quiet moments to write. Yes, I remember the path leading from the Migliera to the Caprile piazza, and the Contadina "reaping and singing by herself". It comes before me as if it were this instant, and that autumnal light. Soon, the wild cyclamens will be blooming again in Capri—and also in Tuscany, and near Rome . . . By the way, if you can manage it while in Rome, I much recommend a brief excursion to the Lake of Nemi, an hour or less drive from Rome, and indescribably moving and beautiful. There is, in the fine little town above the lake, a pleasant restaurant with view over the lake, called Lo Specchio di Diana . . . We hope to go there this time, too.

With most affectionate greetings from us both—Shirley

POSTCARD, NAPLES, JUNE 29, 1993

Dear Donald—Thank you so much for yr extraordinary card (even a cruelly placed postmark cd not obscure the beauty of the stamp of a sagacious portrait—a man wearing a cap that must denote importance: a poet? philosopher?). Here poets are having a rough time—the tombs of Virgil and Leopardi have been brutally attacked. As Henry James said of the death of Rupert Brooke: "<u>Of course</u>." What times, what a weirdo century. There have also been robberies here at the Oriental Institute . . .

[. . .]

Always, with best affection from us both—Shirley

TOKYO, JULY 20, 1993

Dear Shirley,

I was very happy to have your card from Naples. I have been waiting until your return to New York to answer. By all accounts, this is the hottest summer ever in New York. No doubt you attempted to take the first plane to—Omsk? Hudson's Bay? Hammerfest? Japan is still cool, thanks to the rainy season. I wouldn't be much upset if it kept raining without let-up until September. This actually happened a couple of years ago, but I would not wish to deprive Japanese children of their annual week or so of vacation.

I was pleased that you notice the stamp on my card. (I have always delighted in the beautiful Italian stamps you affix to your letters.) The man in the cap is the great haiku poet Bashō. This stamp (along with a good many others) was issued in 1989 to commemorate the journey he took to the north eastern provinces three hundred years earlier. I have mentioned the work based on his journey, The Narrow Road of Oku, in Travelers of a Hundred Ages. Speaking of my books, about ten days ago I received the first copy of the long awaited final volume of my history of Japanese literature, called Seeds in the Heart. It is a great, fat volume of 1300 pages, including an absolutely marvelous index that runs to about 80 pages. It doesn't really seem possible that the book is in being. Every so often each day I feel compelled to hold it and reassure myself that this is not a dream. Publication will be in August, I think, but the publishers, maintaining their tight security, are unlikely to tell anyone until the last moment. But just now I feel so euphoric that I am willing to forgive all the frustration I have experienced. I am glad, too, that they have held down the price to $50. In the past this would not have been a trifling sum even for a book of this size, but nowadays any-thing of a scholarly nature is likely to cost even more, regardless of size.

[. . .]

All my best to you and Francis.
As ever, Donald

TOKYO, AUGUST 27, 1993

Dear Shirley,

I was very glad to receive your letter from New York with the various enclosures.

[. . .]

The articles about the new (actually, old) version of Madame Butterfly intrigued me. I can't remember if I have told you of the Japanese who, more than twenty years ago, visited my office at Columbia with the request that I read the memorial of his grandmother he had written. I was at first disinclined to spend time reading about anybody's grandmother, but I soon discovered that she was rather special. She was the wife of the Japanese ambassador to Italy and a close friend of Puccini's. It was she who transformed the loathsome play by John Luther Long into the perceptive libretto of the opera. When she discovered how Puccini and his librettist had changed the text after the failure of the first version, she refused to attend another performance. Now I know why. I remember my friend's grandmother for another reason. When she was about to leave Italy the queen of Italy gave her a magnificent bracelet. She wore this bracelet when she boarded ship at Naples. On deck, she waved to the Queen, who had gone to see her off, and the bracelet flew into the sea where, I have every reason to believe, it still lodges.

In my last letter I mentioned the publication of the final volume of my history. Publication date was officially August 10, but I've received nothing from the publisher in the way of congratulations, and no one has sent me an advertisement, much less a review. I realized more and more what an extraordinary kindness you showed me in obtaining a review of the book in the <u>New York Times</u>. The attitude of the publisher seems to be fatalistic—it won't sell, so why throw away good money after bad? But my prevailing feeling is still one of joy that, at last, the book is out.

    All my best to you and Francis.
    Yours, Donald

CARD, NEW YORK, DECEMBER 20, 1993

Dear Donald—

Returning to this city, this "season", from the scenes overleaf, we find your kind greeting, your new galleys, and your magnificent volume, concluding the History. How to thank you?—but we do, from the heart and mind; also for the reassurance, the joy really, that such work can still be achieved. As Italians say in such matters, "Facciamo l'impossibile."

[. . .]

A presto—with best affection from Francis and Shirley

TOKYO, AUGUST 29, 1994

Dear Shirley,

How terrible—I have let over three months go by without once writing you. Heaven knows I've thought often of writing, and in fact have composed in my head a number of interesting letters which you will never receive. But I have felt somewhat unsettled and my time has been cut up into odd-shaped fragments. I returned to Japan early this year in order to participate in various publicity events attending the publication of the first volume of the Japanese translation of my history of Japanese literature. The early arrival proved to be effective: I appeared on several television programs (the ultimate way to sell books it would seem), and had photo essays of myself in various magazines. I also gave lectures at places I have already forgotten. This has helped to sell the book (and volume two as well) at a time when serious publications are not selling at all. The Japanese have become frivolous, after all the long centuries of observing Confucian wisdom; no doubt the adverse publicity given abroad to the "rabbit hutches" in which they allegedly live has made the Japanese yearn for the sybaritic delights of the memoirs of TV stars and the like.

I hope that all has been going well with you and Francis. I hear very little from Italy, though I have become more involved than ever with Italian scholarship on Japan. This year the big translation prize is to be awarded to an Italian translation of a modern Japanese literary work. [. . .] I was selected as a judge. I protested that my knowledge of Italian was inadequate even to understand fully surface meanings, let alone judge style, but (I was told) the Italians themselves insisted. They cited the fact that I gave a lecture in Italian on one occasion. I did—but only by burying my nose in the translation made by a friend. I felt rather better when we actually had the meeting of jurors, and I discovered that one of the two Japanese had read less than I! But, as you can imagine, my Italian vocabulary does not include words like _rospo_ for toad or _ravanello_ for radish, but these are precisely the kind of words that appear in a translation of a Japanese story about a peasant family. If only the translations had been of works resembling my beloved opera libretti! A me il ferro! Il mio furor sfuggite invano!

[. . .]

This has been a rather difficult time for me. I'm treated extremely well even by people I hardly know, so I can't possibly complain; but I sense a growing distance between my old friends and myself, not hostility of course, but each of them in his own way shutting himself up in his family or his work the kind of preparation for the final cocoon. Last week I almost got around to persuading myself that I should really return to New York, but I suppose that this problem is not peculiar to the Japanese. This momentary crisis was provoked when, after relating to my oldest friend here my current difficulties with Mrs. Mishima (who has always been ready to believe the worst of me because I did not abandon all other work to translate her husband's novels) he commented that he sympathized with Mrs.

Mishima. Of course, I sympathized with her when her husband killed himself, and I sympathized with her when her son ran away. But these are events of twenty years ago and do not really justify her rage when she decides, without giving me a chance to defend myself, that I have done something wrong. I suppose I was most upset by my friend's objectivity. I can imagine how you would react if you heard that Mrs. Mishima had been making false accusations. Or her declaration to mutual acquaintances that she could not excuse my failure to attend her father's funeral, regardless of the circumstances (I was in hospital).

These minor events do not justify the discontent and even anxiety I feel some of the time, but they may explain why it has been diffi-cult to feel composed enough to write a letter. Quite apart from such personal matters, I have also experienced difficulty getting underway with my next book, a biography of the Emperor Meiji. I have a great deal of material in hand, but I still haven't found the man, and per-haps never will. Is it because, despite his fame, he was really colorless and uninteresting? Or have I simply not yet found the needed docu-ments that will unlock the mystery?

Though I probably do not deserve it, I will be very happy to have a letter from you telling me about what you have been doing in Italy and New York.

As ever,
Donald

ROME, SEPTEMBER 16, 1994

Dear Donald—

Your letter, moving and to me especially poignant, arrived just as we were leaving New York for—as you see—first, Rome and now, tomorrow, Naples. In the onslaught of preparations for departure and above all of dealing with the volume of impersonal details that now fall exclusively to me to "resolve", it maddened me to be unable to send you even so brief a word as this, <u>ad interim</u> because I want to try to reach you before you leave Japan for Italy. When you arrive here, we shall indeed be in Naples (or rather, probably, in Capri where I'll be "attending"—that is, briefly looking in on—a very interesting conference of historians about Tiberius: new documents, in fact incised bronze tablets, have been discovered in Spain dramatically bearing on Tiberius' arranged murder of Germanicus and then of Gnaeus Piso, his instrument; these more than validate the drastic narrative in the Annals of Tacitus—an account long disputed as too condemnatory of Tiberius and now seen to be if anything over-lenient). It would be utterly frustrating to think you were in Rome and we could not meet. Please do telephone us and let us know when you arrive and where you'll be staying. [. . .] I had many thoughts and impressions on reading your letter, and shall—if I may—indulge them at length when I know that a letter will reach you. My anxiety now is to get this word into the post promptly. [. . .] As to your experiences with long and trusted friends, how disheartening these things are, even a moment's wanton hostility seeming to shake the affections and associations of years. Bad enough in one's youth, but searing as one grows older. The behaviour of your "oldest friend" (related to the caprices of Mishima's widow) might seem incomprehensible entirely were it not for the first section of your letter, which seemed to me to have a possible bearing on it: you mentioned the reception, splendid and so merited, of your history of Japanese literature in its Japanese translation. Is not this a possible cause of your friend's antagonism?—alas, even better natures can give way to jealousy and resentment in such situations. <u>Così, purtroppo, l'essere umano.</u> Forgive my suggesting this if it is wide of the mark; but at least among occidentals it is a common reaction to "success". Crowned with the laurel, Petrarch said: "the laurel brought me much envy, and did nothing to further my gift."

I must run to the post office—San Silvestro—now with this. I wish I knew where to reach you when you arrive in Rome. [...] With all affection and solidarity—Shirley

NAPLES, NOVEMBER 8, 1994[6]

Dear Donald—

I have been thinking of you so much. If I'd had your number I would have telephoned you. It's only now that I have consistent time to write letters—and I am so grateful for yours, and for your generous and truthful words. You are a person who can be generous and truthful together, something rare.

Francis was, as one of the obituaries from England said, "a man of great sweetness and great strength"—again not a common combination. He had no vanity, and no unkindness. Literature and art were for him immediate and joyful. In the last year or two he would look with even more than usual attention at rare book catalogues that are sent to us, and one day he said to me: "I would like to send for all of these books, really", and laughed—meaning, to have enough life ahead to have "lu tous les livres" . . . You know how he admired you, and what pleasure he had in your friendship. I smiled at his highest accolade—that he wished you lived in our building. He forgot many things in the last months, but he never forgot to be himself, or to enjoy the company of his friends. Of that unforgettable evening at Columbia he said, quite recently, "It was perfect." On the night itself, when we were coming back from your celebration in a taxi, he said, "There can be no envy of something so rightful."

These days are for me a series of contrasting moods and impressions—sometimes realising, sometimes disbelieving. It seems to me a year since 20th October. I've just returned from Florence, where I went for John Pope-Hennessey's funeral. Harold Acton, John, Francis—these three were long friends, and all have departed within a year. Singular spirits, from a world where singularity was possible and unselfconscious. I feel, like Yeats,

"that Time may bring

Approved patterns of women or of men,

But not that selfsame excellence again."

I will return to NYC as planned, about 2 December. I look forward immensely to your own return there. I too "wish we lived in the same building"; but I feel that we do in a metaphorical sense. Yes, it was beautiful that we had been reading A[ntony] and C[leopatra] the day before his death. Sometimes he would say, "Let's read this last scene over at once," or "Think of being the person who could write this"—of a particular line or phrase. Just as ever.

Let us be in touch before NYC. Thank you again for your affection, dear Donald, and your kindness in your words about me, and for the warmth of your remembrance. This brings every affectionate thought

from

Shirley

TOKYO, JULY 21, 1995

Dear Shirley,

It has been months since we last saw each other, but I feel as if, mysteriously, we have been in touch throughout. In the case of some friends, a lapse in correspondence might make it difficult to resume the friendship, but I don't think that could happen to us. All the same, when I catch myself hoping for a letter from you as I open the post box, I realized that in order to receive such a letter I must do something about it!

My stay in Japan this time has been taken up largely with writing the biography of the Emperor Meiji. Yesterday I completed the installment of the serial for December. This should put me well ahead of the game, but my translator can devote full time to my work only during the summer, and I therefore must accumulate a considerable backlog. I have found writing the biography much more enjoyable than I had anticipated, though it is hard work. The hardest part is reading the documents. Although the materials I have been using were written mainly in the 1860s, they are written in a language which is definitely not modern Japanese nor classical Japanese either. The closest thing I can think of would be reading a document composed in rebuses with pictures of an eye and of the sea used in order to convey "I see." That's not quite it, but I can't think of a better parallel. The next hardest part is even more exasperating. Japanese historians rarely give sources, and this means I must comb through likely books, none of them possessing an index, for a reference.

But I suppose this weird detective work is part of the attraction of doing the work. I desire like St George to plant my foot on the neck of the slain dragon, though I am afraid that this particular dragon is stronger than I.

How have you been, Shirley? I imagine that, even with all your friends, you have missed Francis every day. Perhaps you have found consolation in your work. I hope so. I should be in New York briefly in August and shall try to get in touch with you. [. . .] I hope we can meet.

As ever, Donald

POSTCARD, NAPLES, SEPTEMBER 16, 1995

Dear Donald—here is a house[7] you may have missed in your Brazilian adventures. And the—really, excellent, I think—review of Mishima's drama which I snatched up from the living room sofa as I left our NYC apt for the airport. How infinitely <u>busy</u> one always is these days. After fine days in Rome, I'm beside the sea at Posillipo, and soon to go to Capri. And glad to find that I've already resumed my work here. Lily asks me, When is Donald next coming to Naples? I wish I knew.

As you had other islands on your mind in 1943, perhaps the name of Pantellería—on one of these stamps—strikes no chord with you? I was eleven, I think, when the "Allies" invaded that hot little place as a first step to the Sicilian landings . . . It's now a resort, inevitably.

How good, such a bonus, to see you in New York—I enjoyed each moment—with all affection—Shirley

TOKYO, OCTOBER 31, 1995

Dear Shirley,

The end of another month. I remember in the past desiring nothing more than that time would pass quickly so that some impatiently awaited event would be imminent; but now I begrudge each month that passes. Perhaps that is natural at my age, though I confess it takes some effort to persuade myself that I really am 73. When I see someone on the street who is more or less my own age, that fact never occurs to me; instead, I think, "That old man!"

All of which is the preamble to expressing my grief that I have allowed so much time to elapse before acknowledging the review of the Mishima play that you so kindly sent. The review is indeed splendid. When the same play was first performed in New York many years ago, just once as an experiment, the critics deplored its old-fashioned theatricality, and declared that no American audience could accept a play in which the main action occurs off stage, out of sight of the audience. This was probably why it was not performed a second time. But the fault, as we know now, was not in the play but in the direction—and in the critics.

I have just finished reading Francis's <u>A Woman, A Man, and Two Kingdoms</u>. What a wonderfully civilized book this is! It is a joy both in the conception and in the beautiful translations of the letters. I'm glad to know these two people, and I feel quite certain that I would have heard of neither without Francis's book. The first book of his I ever read was <u>Flaubert and Madame Bovary</u>. I remember buying this as an undergraduate, at a time when I could afford few books apart from Everyman's and The Modern Library. I wonder what happened to my copy. In which change of address did it get lost or stolen? Or perhaps it was a visitor who admired it so much I gave it away. That was at least 55 years ago.

My own work progresses slowly but surely. The only problem is that I still don't know where I am going! My hero is still only 16 and has not yet said one word, at least not in my hearing. Will I really have the energy and devotion to pursue him to the bitter end at the age of 60? This evening I was asked by an editor to write a biography of Mishima. That won't be easy either, if I accept.

I hope all goes well with you. Please write when you can. As ever,
Donald

The magnificent Italian stamps gave the envelope a special aura. Yes, to answer your questions, I remember Pantellería very well. Also, Balikpapan and Babelthuap.

CAPRI, NOVEMBER 29, 1995

Dear Donald—

Thank you so much for your letter, more than ever welcome while I'm dismantling our Capri flat and feeling in the process dismantled in myself. The tasks are of course indescribably boring; the spiritual effects are harrowing. In about five days, I leave these rooms forever—in fact, the rooms (providentially) will cease to exist, since the Legree-like landlords mean to "restructure" the place, adding illicit offshoots here and there. I'm glad that in this way the place ceases with our occupancy.

How good, what you say about Francis' Galiani & Mme d'Épinay book. I felt about it just what you say—that I would never have known those two without his having done that work. Makes one wonder—as so often—what else of fascination and power is lying under one's nose. Supposing I'd been sent by the UN to Istanbul in 1956, rather than to Naples—I'd have known another fascinating and incorrigible city; and not known Naples. Well, I shd not include you in such reflections, you being a mild-mannered polymath with "thoughts that wander through eternity" . . . I wonder if you've decided to write on Mishima?—speaking for myself, I hope so. As to the Meiji, one trusts to your powers. Has anyone else—in Japan or elsewhere—written at length on him?

I must give you, when we are reunited in New York in January, a new copy of Francis' "Flaubert and Madame Bovary", to replace the fifty-five year old copy. (There is a recent new paperback.) In Scott Fitzgerald's published letters (Penguin ed.), there is a letter of 1938 to a friend in which he lists four or five books that have been important to him in recent years. One is "Flaubert & Mme Bovary", after which he writes: "Absolute tops". Another is Kafka's "The Trial", recently appearing in English. I forget the rest at this moment. When

I showed that to Francis some years ago, he said, "Oh, if I'd known of this at the time, what it wd have meant to me."

I must see what stamps I have in this derelict apartment, to put on the envelope. Your own Japanese stamp was very fine—it made me think of Ivan's screen . . . Next year it will be twenty years since his death. Waste, sadness, tragedy . . . The Basho Stamp you once sent was delightful.

With fits of storm, the season here goes on very beautifully. Only the nights are cold, and I turn on the heating. The early dark—at about 4:00 PM—is the killer. The mornings often radiant and warm, and I go out without a coat. Brilliant sunshine—still many flowers in Capri, and almost no people. [. . .] My work, essential to my survival these days, has been engulfed by this business of leaving the Capri place, which occupies my days and nights. However, I've done a fair bit, and hope to get much onto paper in NY this winter. The absence of Francis, and his presence in all our rooms—including the room where I write this, with all its memories and experience—continues inconceivable, always more realised and disbelieved. In these experiences one feels very close to one's own death and in differing ways. Forgive melancholy observations.

How I do look forward to your return. No cherry blossom was ever, I'm sure, more welcome than your January arrival. We'll be in touch meantime, and I send this with the warmest wishes and affection—Shirley

TOKYO, JUNE 24, 1996

Dear Shirley,

This letter must begin (as so many of my letters do) with an apology—in this case, for not having got in touch with you during my recent visit to Italy. I certainly thought of it often, but chiefly when I was in a car in some remote part of southeastern Italy, or when I was attending a moderately interesting conference in Venice. But I generally was too exhausted in the evenings to attempt to make a call. I do apologize.

Puglia proved to be quite marvelous. I think the single most impressive site was for me the cathedral at Trani, almost on the water's edge. But I shall remember too Martina Franca, an eighteenth-century town with hardly a false note, and the weird architecture at Alberobello. The last-named place has become very touristy. At the hotel I was astonished to see a Japanese tour group of some twenty or thirty people. The Japanese were completely inoffensive, but I hadn't expected them!

[. . .]

From Italy I flew to New York, spent two days there and then flew to Tokyo. If I hadn't had so many books etc. to take to Japan I could have flown to Tokyo from Milan. I arrived here exhausted & remained exhausted during a protracted cold that caused incessant coughing. I had not realized before how tiring it is to cough.

The rainy season has started. It doesn't rain all the time, but it is never clear for a whole day. I have various tedious things to do— prefaces for books by friends, recommendations, predictions for the twenty-first century. I'm happy that I have a major project—the biography of the Emperor Meiji. If I didn't have that I would certainly feel that my time was being frittered away.

Last week I had my birthday. I find it absolutely incredible that I am seventy-four. Why am I not filled with wisdom? But, in another sense, I know just how old I am from the people I can remember distinctly who died long ago. Yes, I tell myself, I knew Bertrand Russell. Yes, I heard Toscanini conduct, and I saw Flagstad & Melchior in Tristan und Isolde. But that part of me has so much less reality than the adolescent still wondering if he said the wrong thing, if he should have sent a birthday card or given the waiter a bigger tip.

I trust that your new house is coming along well. I think I told you, but I bought another apartment in the same building in Tokyo. It was filthy, but it is now transformed into something like elegance! I am sure the Italian workmen can do no less.

As always, Donald.

NEW YORK, AUGUST 3, 1996

Dear Donald—

[. . .]

Thank you so much for your delightful, interesting, touching letter. I thought of you when (I thought) you wd be in Puglia. Yes, what a strange in some ways outlandish and yet ancient and fascinating territory. Everett Fahy promises me that next time he comes to Naples he will take a few days so that he and I can drive there—he knows it well; I haven't been for many years. And fear to see again the trulli, which I'm told are dishearteningly exploited, like so many Uncle Tom's Original Cabins. But—Lecce, Otranto, Trani . . . Martina Franca . . . in late years I was often nagging Francis to abandon Flaubert, or Galiani, for a few days so that we cd go there again together. But then it became too onerous to suggest to him. He had consecrated his energies to getting those two lost books finished, realising that memory and concentration were beginning to fail him. When we were in New York, he would go back to his desk after dinner, having worked the whole day but being unwilling to lose the added time in the evening. I don't know if I showed you his last piece of published writing—in the TLS just a year before his death—a review of the last two volumes of collected letters of Proust, edited by Philip Kolb. Beautiful piece of writing, unbearably so to me. I wd like to have a rather brief book eventually of selected short pieces by Francis, and that wd be one of them. Well, I cannot tell you how excruciating it is to me to be without him; and to find him everywhere. Not something that can change; not something one wants to change.

When we meet, I'd like to know whether, on that last tiring day of your drive up to the Adriatic, you stopped even briefly at Recanati—the native "paese" of Leopardi, where the beautiful palazzo of his family presides over the town, where—despite some bumbling provincial exploitation of this "asset"—the place remains as he immortalised it, fairly breathing out his suffering there, his ecstasy over the surrounding countryside and the sea, in short his genius. Did I mention that we have friends (in Rome) whose family seat is at Fano?—delightful town, where we visited them abt seven years ago. Their palazzo incorporates the arch of Augustus, which is the gate of the town. I find the countryside of the Marche wonderfully beautiful, much of it as Tuscany was before commerce and Chiantishire set up so many signals.

You are the only friend I have who had to fly from Italy to New York to pick up some books on the way to Japan. I hope your cough has left you—a constant cough is nightmarish, one can't sleep. There are drops—as you doubtless know—that "soothe" (ie, partially paralyse) the throat and on drastic occasions they are worth having.

Here too it's the rainy season, virtually oriental. (Oh, how I remember those Hong Kong rains, I can smell them and I can see the lurid green of the Peak—when it was visible—mouldering in the wet.) Even in NY there are pockets of mouldy damp—in a cupboard left closed for more than a day or two, for instance. I don't recall such a wet summer here. For myself, I don't mind; anything but that unspeakable heat. But it is curious.

Warm wishes—Shirley

NAPLES, OCTOBER 21, 1996

Dear Donald—thank you so much for your kind and beautiful letter, and for your postcard (the postcard having come with excruciating delay). A propos excruciating delay: it's mortifying to me that you should again be sending word, magnanimously, when I have been musing unachieved letters to you for weeks. Please never imagine that you of all people could ever write what would "annoy" me. Such a fatality is, from my point of view, inconceivable, <u>assolutamente esclusa</u>. (But how strange that such a possibility does enter one's head or not hearing from a friend; precariousness of even best affection seems unassuageable—unless I suppose for those without imagination.)

Let me also thank you for the stamp of a cat—a cat whose naturally slit eyes seem to have an oriental obliqueness in this case; to which a Japanese stamp designer is of course entitled. (Some animals curiously do look national: impossible to imagine a scotty dog of any other origin.) So there are orange cats in Japan—I try to remember if cats known to me in Japanese graphics have been as orange as this, and with white muzzle. Perhaps the occupation was responsible for the marmalade tinge?—a revenge on the yellow peril. What we have all lived through. The miraculous Noh mask has the same feline form of eyes. Extraordinary object. Once I talked with Ivan about the—shockingly, to westerners—cosmetically black teeth. No doubt the rotting teeth of prominent ladies at court played some part in the phenomenon as it appears in art?—as scalp diseases, and baldness, and prematurely grey hair of court men and women precipitated wigs and powdered hair in France and England (powder must have fallen over their velvet clothes in unlovely manner). Did you ever see Rossellini's wonderful film, La Prise de Pouvoir about the young Louis Quatorze?—rare depiction of a historical theme that made one feel one was witnessing something like true life, true atmosphere.

The strangeness, the monstrous dress, the bizarre formalities were pervasive but incidental—never insisted on by the director, never "featured". It was the first half of a pair of films that Rossellini made for television, sometimes now shown in cinemas. RR died before he could make the second part. The imagination for a past existence was remarkable. Analogous perhaps to the Gate of Hell.

[. . .]

Talking abt your work on the Emperor Meiji to Bill Maxwell, I said, if I think of what is involved in such work, "I feel that the life of a novelist, writing in one's own language, is a sinecure." Bill said that he knew you would "feel yourself into that man", and that the result would be another revelation. I wonder if you think of the work that way?—I know that Francis did "feel himself into" his biographical subject, not because he came to sympathise with them in every way but in a state of attention and imagination. He said once that one's discoveries could only come in that way. And now I find in yr letter something of the same "condition"—that your sympathy for the period increases, and that the intimate details emerge . . .

Yes, I recall that Francis said he wished you lived in our building. I wish the same. Yesterday was the second anniversary of his death. Painful hours. Yet with a sense of being close to him, to our life; and that is precious to me.

When we meet, I'll offer you my own experience of being a property owner (few cubic metres). My little place looks beautiful. But the torrential rains have prevented it from being dried and aired, so I'll not be able to move in until I return in mid-November. My hope is that you will see it one day. Meantime, I'm surrounded by boxes of books at Naples, and things things things that should move back to Capri. Things do take over if they get a chance.

With all affection, with every good wish and thought—looking forward to our reunion—Shirley

3

1997–2008

TOKYO, JUNE 22, 1997

Dear Shirley,

It is hard to believe how quickly time has passed since I saw you last in Naples. I enjoyed the evening at that wonderful house overlooking Vesuvius in the Bay. I have been most remiss in not writing you sooner to express my thanks. I have no excuse to offer. Although I think of you very often and I have decided many times that tomorrow I shall definitely write you, there are always deadlines of one sort or another. Today, for example, there is a long translation into Japanese of an episode I have written on the life of the Emperor Meiji. Naturally, the translator wants it back instantly, but this time I have the courage to say "No! I am writing Shirley."

I remained in New York somewhat later than usual. I can't remember if I have told you, but I was given an honorary degree by Columbia. It is unusual for a university to give an honorary degree to one of its own who already has a doctor's degree, but I appreciated the exception made in this case. The ceremony took place on the 21st of May. This was the same day as the annual festivities at the Academy, and this meant that I had half my lunch at Columbia and half at the Academy. I had to attend the Academy because I was the sponsor for admission as a foreign member of Ōe Kenzaburō. My relations with him have been incomprehensible to me—sometimes he is extremely friendly, sometimes icily remote—but I certainly did not wish him to think I was avoiding a ceremony at which he was honored. I was glad I went. He was in unusually high spirits and everything went well.

The Blashfield address, given by Margaret Drabble, was well written, but left little impression. She decried the commercialization of the English countryside, not a startling point of view, and ended up with admiration for Rushdie, which everybody shares. But at least it was enjoyable as it was delivered.

I returned to Japan in time to serve as a judge of a translation prize sponsored by Shizuoka Prefecture. Candidates were required to translate one of a selection of literary works and one of a similar selection of criticism. Translations were surprisingly good, and I felt pleased to have participated in awarding the prize.

The return to Japan this time has been a strange and even painful experience. I have two especially close friends, both about my age. One, who was largely responsible for launching my literary career here, died in April. The other, who became my friend about a month after I first arrived in Kyoto in 1953 and has remained unusually close, is now in extremely fragile health, and (worse, as far as I am concerned) he no longer seems to be the same person. He fortunately has a devoted family, who take his remoteness in their stride, but it is extremely painful for me to spend time with him, remembering how our conversation always leapt ahead with too many things to say for their ever being said.

I have even thought of curtailing my visits to Japan. This is strange, especially because last year I acquired a second apartment as a place to work. I like being in Japan, of course, but I have not been successful in forming new friendships, though I am also still in demand for lectures, articles, reviews, and even photographs of me at work, eating, or simply genially smiling at the camera. This attention is not only flattering but makes the rest of my time all the more valuable. In New York, the alternative, I have a few extremely precious friends, naturally including you, but they tend to be busy and it is not always easy to meet them. My trouble, as is apparent to me even as I write these words, is that I have been too fortunate. I have lost my two closest friends here, but I remain in good health. I have delightful places to live in two countries, and lead extremely agreeable lives in both. I can hear from somewhere a harsh voice, probably with a New York accent, saying, "What are _you_ complaining about?"

The other night I went to a production of <u>Coriolanus</u> done by an English company. I think you would have loathed it. The director, who was also the main actor, is called Stephen Berkoff. He has decided that Coriolanus was a fascist, and communicated this belief at the end of one scene by having Coriolanus and his henchman perform a goose step as they leave. The production, in the modern manner, had no scenery and the actors all wore scruffy business suits. Berkoff himself was hard to understand because he gabbled his words, but he seems to have decided to enhance his part by eliminating one important character. (I hope I remember to enclose the statement inserted in the program.) And yet, despite everything, the play was intermittently moving. Even though it was not Shakespeare, it was well choreographed, and when the other actors and actresses spoke, one caught something of the original play. If I were terribly rich I would stage <u>Coriolanus</u> exactly as written, just to prove what really needs no proving, that Shakespeare was a lot more intelligent than his modern adapters.

I hope that all goes well with you. I expect to be in New York briefly at the end of October. Will you be there? I hope so!

As ever, Donald

TOKYO, JULY 30, 1997

Dear Shirley,

[. . .]

There is not much to report. I have been extremely busy, but almost always at the same thing, looking for materials concerning the Emperor Meiji and writing about what I find. I have also written a small number of miscellaneous pieces for newspapers and magazines, but (mercifully!) I have not had to deliver any lectures. This summer promises to be rainy. I prefer rain to heat, but there is somewhere in the back of my head a remembrance of golden summer days, such as I have rarely experienced, and this makes me less appreciative than I should be for the gloomy skies.

There doesn't seem to be much likelihood of returning to Italy this year. I have been asked if I would give a paper on shoes in Japanese literature at a conference sponsored by Ferragamo, but Japanese literature is notoriously deficient in descriptions of shoes. I'm afraid I lack the courage (effrontery?) to give an hour's address on the subject, though I would like to visit Italy again.

[. . .]

All my best wishes.
As ever, Donald

SYDNEY, AUGUST 16, 1997

Dear Donald—

As you see, I'm a few miles closer (or so I think?) to you. I can't thank you enough for your two letters, and for being so thoughtful as to write to me the second time on not hearing. Your first letter reached me with some delay—NOT because of your having sent it to Italy, but because the main post office at Naples (a huge bombé fascist affair that is now admired for its modern architecture . . . such is our contemporary desperation) was being painted, inside, and no mail was being sorted or delivered. A Neapolitan detail. The letter reached me shortly before I left for NY, where I intended to answer it right away—then I was swallowed up in writing my speech for Australia, which I gave here three evenings ago. The speech terrorised me—I couldn't get close to my theme, rewrote continually, felt desperate towards the institute that was bringing me so expensively to Sydney . . . That continued to the evening before my departure, when I stayed up most of the night to recast the talk, which only then seemed to me fairly tolerable. Then—the long, long flight in the dark, wondering why I had ever got into it all. Arrived at Sydney at dawn, a beautiful day coming up, to be met by Ann Lewis, whose house and boat you'll remember—so kind. Since then, a week ago, every "midwinter" day has been like early summer, and with an inexpressibly beautiful clear light. People have been immensely kind. Many things have got better at Sydney (and some things, of course, worse). The great relief: the "speech" went very well (a dinner for 600 people—politics, corporations, the arts), such an accessible, responsive audience. To my astonishment, I had a lovely evening.

[. . .]

Your description of your changed situation in Japan—with the infirmity and death of friends—is so real to me. It is what Francis experienced with Paris, after a lifetime attachment to the city and to his friends there. When he finished his book on Cocteau, in 1970, we had been living in Paris part of the year for five years. We knew many people, had also met many people through the Cocteau connection—fascinating, every one of them—yet Francis decided that we wd pursue our Italian life, and make sporadic visits to France. Because his friends in Paris from the 1930s, all older than he, were disappearing one by one; and the new friends made through Cocteau were also for the most part elderly and starting to drop away. He felt that the city for him wd be a haunted place; and the modern changes dismayed him—skyscrapers, a new hardness . . . Of course we re-visited the city, but never lived there again. I don't think, of course, that your "case" is just like that. But the cruel feeling of a chapter closing, of the evaporation of visible evidence of one's memories seems something analogous. As you say, we've been so fortunate—but how to settle, now, for less in these beloved and familiar places? Again fortunately, we don't yet have to make definite decisions. Of course, selfishly, I'll be very pleased if you decide to spend more time in New York. But how good if "things" could go on for us without those sad mutations. And how grateful one is to have one's work, what one has chosen, and wished, to do.

Sydney is full of memories for me while I'm here. I think little about these things while I'm in New York or Italy. The light here is itself poignant and evocative to me, recalling childhood mornings and afternoons (at that age, evenings didn't play such a role). Huge changes—and then some salient things utterly unaltered.

[. . .]

Coriolanus—how glad I am not to have seen what you describe. It is a marvellous play. Francis and I would read it aloud with excitement. Uncompromising. When I first came to NY—with my parents, at the beginning of the 1950s—a friend invited me to go to a production of Coriolanus at the Phoenix theatre, then down on First Ave about 20th St. The actor was Robert Ryan, whom I'd seen in films. It was splendid—the simple, faithful production and the wonderful acting. (I don't suppose his mother's name really was Volumina—a stroke of Shakespeare's genius. However, I'll look in Petrarch.) Ryan was a very tall craggy man, highly trained stage actor originally—and the performance was unforgettable. Many years later Francis and I were at Marya Mannes' apt in the Dakota, and Ryan, a neighbour in the building, came in for a drink—v civil and pleasant person. I asked him about the 1952 *Coriolanus* and he said it was one of the best experiences of his acting life.

I beg your pardon for this rambling letter, which I now confide to the Pacific posts. We'll be in touch—and I so look forward to Oct-Nov days in New York. Also, something to tell you about "my" Villa dei Papiri at Herculaneum—Good news there.

With all affection, and with apologies for delay—Shirley.

TOKYO, SEPTEMBER 19, 1997

Dear Shirley,

I was very happy to receive your letter from Sydney. The envelope festooned with rare and curious denizens of land and sea. I think you will be glad to know that when two English princes, sons of Edward VII, visited the Japanese court in 1881 they gave the Empress two wallabies they had acquired in Australia, assuring her that the animals would make the palace just as cheery as their ship. The younger Prince, then only 16, had dragons tattooed on both arms. Does that sound like George V to you?

I never really expect a letter to Naples will reach its destination without delay. I remember well the huge, ugly post office. During my last visit to Naples I stayed at the Hotel Oriente (appropriately!) which is just across the street from the post office, I think, though, that the worst example of fascist architecture is the Milan railway station. No doubt it, too, is admired.

[...]

My main work, the biography of the Emperor Meiji, has been proceeding satisfactorily. It may, when finished three or four years from now, be the best biography ever written of a Japanese emperor. But the things I don't know and should know are maddeningly obvious.

I have only a few crumbs of what might be called individuality to offer my readers. I have just found a most remarkable bit of information. In 1883, for no reason I can think of, he refused to see his advisers, did not participate in meetings where his presence was needed, and so on. When Queen Victoria withdrew completely from governmental work, this can be ascribed to grief over Prince Albert's death. But <u>why</u> did Meiji refuse to see even the ministers he most trusted? Someone must have known, but perhaps out of constraint over revealing royal secrets never wrote anything. I am lucky to have this piece of information about his withdrawal. Although it is not a secret, it has never been used by historians. Probably because it cannot be verified.

[. . .]

I am sure that your talk was wonderful, and hope that you will include it in a volume of talks, including those in Italian. I remember so well that beautiful talk you gave at my retirement party at Columbia. It was the high point of the occasion. You asked me to shoot you if you ever again contemplate making a speech. No, I will not shoot you, but (if you like) I will exclude everyone from the audience except myself.

I shall write again to New York as the date of my return approaches. In the meantime, I hope that the weather in Capri is perfect & that you are enjoying it.

As ever, Donald

TOKYO, DECEMBER 23, 1997

Dear Shirley,

Yesterday I received your Christmas card. Of course, I was happy to receive it, but I was startled and dismayed to learn that you had spent the autumn in New York having an operation. If we were living in the world of literature, as opposed to the real world, I should certainly have sensed something even without hearing from you; but when

I thought of you (which was often) I always imagined you reading a book on a terrace overlooking the scenery at Capri or Naples. I hope you have fully recovered.

I have news which is at once very good but also disappointing. I have been planning to return to New York on January 12, but I had word that I have received the Asahi Prize. This is an important prize awarded not only to persons concerned with literature but to scientists, economists and so on. The announcement is made on New Year's Day, but I have had word from the newspaper that makes the award. My first thought (apart from joy!) was that I would fly back to New York as planned, then return for the ceremony, which takes place on January 30. But then I began to think of three trans-Pacific flights in two weeks. This is not nearly as long as the flight to Sydney, but it is exhausting. [. . .]

The autumn was truly exhausting. I gave lectures in a dozen or more places, each one entailing not only the actual hour and a half of talking, standard in Japan, but the reception afterwards and—horrors—the innumerable commemorative photographs, each preceded by the command "Cheese!" Naturally, the lecturing interfered with my writing. I now have quite a lot of money, most of it subject to heavy taxes, and memories of the ride from the station or airport to the site of the lecture, normally all I see of any town.

[. . .]

All my warmest greetings, Donald

TOKYO, JULY 21, 1998

Dear Shirley,

Thank you for your Donizetti card, festooned as always with beautiful Italian postage stamps. I stopped saving stamps at the age of 17 or 18, but I retain affection for them, whether beautiful ones such as those you always put on letters from Italy or old ones showing Franz Joseph, Edward VII, Queen Wilhemina. I feel nostalgia when I see their faces. As a child I was a passionate royalist and could not get interested in American history for this reason. My greatest favorite was Marie Antoinette and I kept reading about her in the hopes that in the next history I read she would escape. It did not occur to me that all histories would tell the same story.

During the last week or so I have made a painful historical discovery. About thirty years ago I wrote a long article about the cultural effects in Japan of the Sino-Japanese War of 1894–5. What I wrote was not mistaken, but I now know how much I did not write. My interest was in the prints, poems, songs, plays and so on that came out of the war, but now that I am writing something closer to a history I have to examine the battles too. The massacre at Port Arthur, which I vaguely knew about, on close look is horrifying. In terms of the number of people killed, it naturally does not rival what one well-placed bomb achieved in World War II, but there is a difference that I cannot easily explain between the action of a man pressing a button releasing a gigantic bomb, and a band of soldiers swooping down on unarmed people and slashing off their heads. This may simply be a failure of the imagination, but perhaps it is something worse. As an intelligent English or American reporter commented in 1894, if a stalwart troop of soldiers from one of the Western democracies broke into a crowd of dusky people and slaughtered them, people reading about this were likely to shrug this off, taking it for granted that savages must be taught they have to obey the rules of civilization; in this case, however, because the sword-wielding soldiers were Japanese, their action was taken as proof that, for all their show of modernity, they were fundamentally barbarians. I shall have to describe the events as I now see them. Perhaps they are not really necessary to a biography of the Emperor Meiji, who was many miles away and probably never learned what had happened. But, knowing the facts, and remembering how cheerfully I wrote about the war thirty years ago, I feel obliged to record them.

Although this kind of research can be depressing (as in the present instance), on the whole I enjoy it extremely. I am bombarded with requests for lectures, articles, interviews, dialogues, roundtable discussions and so on. This attention is highly flattering, and I should probably miss it if it stopped altogether. But I yearn to be back at my musty old books, in the hopes of discovering one tiny germ of new knowledge.

I imagine that you are back in New York now, fleeing the merriment of the August holidays. Oddly for me, I rather wish I were back in New York. It is not exactly the case that the charm of Japan has worn off. There is still much that gives me pleasure. But, having attained a few weeks ago my 76th birthday, I have been thinking of what I want to do most during my remaining years, and the answer is simply: work. I have become a workaholic! Seriously, apart from the great pleasure of being with friends like you, I derive the most satisfaction from reading, perhaps finding a fact that has escaped attention, and trying to make sense of it. This is, I now see, better done in New York than here, where I must fend off friendly, generous people who want me to do something which may not take much trouble but which I don't really want to do.

[. . .]

As ever, Donald

TOKYO, SEPTEMBER 23, 1998

Dear Shirley,

I haven't heard from you in a few months, and naturally I worry. I hope that you have simply been too busy with your present work to write a letter. Or perhaps my letter never reached you, a possibility that one must take seriously these days. I still look forward each day to the delivery of mail, but even if the box is full of postal matter, it rarely contains any letters. The telephone, fax machines, e-mail and Heavens knows what else have combined to destroy or at least submerge the letter as a means of communication. Can you imagine Clarissa writing an e-mail missive as she is being carried off by that dreadful Mr. Lovelace?

I believe that you mentioned you would return to New York in order to be present at the celebration of Bill Maxwell's ninetieth birthday. I wish I could be there too. I have just finished reading his novel <u>A Folded Leaf</u>. I found it almost unbearably moving. He writes so beautifully and with such truth. And also with the humor which, I suppose, is a necessary part of any work in the English language. Please send him my warm regards when you see him.

I have been slowly but steadily moving ahead with my biography of the Emperor Meiji. I remember someone—I think it was Leon Edel—saying that one must fall in love with the subject of a biography. I am afraid I haven't managed to fall in love with Meiji, but quite clearly he doesn't want my love. He never did anything despotic, never ordered the deaths of innocent people. Nor, for that matter, did he allow any statue to be erected of himself on or off a horse, though others of the time were so honored. But except for brief flashes of temper, which he usually regretted the next day, his voice is never heard. If he had not lived in an incredibly interesting period, it would be hard to know what to write about him. I have had little reaction to the three and a half years of the biography, as serialized in a Japanese magazine, but it is too late to turn back now!

I really don't know where to send this letter, but I suppose (on the basis of my experience with Mussolini's post office in Naples) that New York is safer. New York safe? Well, not really! Best wishes as always,

Yours, Donald

TOKYO, JULY 22, 1999

Dear Shirley,

Just typing the figure 1999 seems somehow ominous, doesn't it? Today I saw a BBC television program about people who think that the world will end next year. One man warned solemnly that this is our last chance to flee from the doomed planet earth. He didn't say where he advised us to go instead; perhaps he doesn't want his extra-terrestrial haven becoming overcrowded!

Last night I had a dream which ended with you urging me to go to Reggio Emilia. Of course, I'm always ready to go anywhere you recommend, but before I could find out <u>why</u> I should go there, I woke up. My plans are still not definite; perhaps I shall investigate Reggio Emilia. Unfortunately, I don't even know what I should be looking for—buildings, landscapes, gardens, food, wine, music???

I arrived in Japan on June 6th after a voyage from San Francisco. An airplane journey of two days, as you know, can be excruciating, but on the sea I found myself wishing the journey were longer. Nothing special happened, and apart from a one-day stop in Honolulu there were not any variations in the scenery, but it was wonderful being completely in control of my time. No, that was not really true. There were prescribed meal times, and I had two lectures to give. But these were insignificant interruptions to the hours when I read or, for exercise, strolled along the deserted decks. Since arriving in Japan I have been following my usual routine, a mixture of serious study, lectures on topics that don't interest me anymore but seem to interest audiences, and a small amount of seeing friends. So many friends have either died or are no longer what they were. That is the price one pays for living to be 77. There is a chance I may visit Italy for a week or so in November. There is to be another conference in Venice on Hokusai. I am not being modest when I say that I have nothing new to contribute on the subject of Hokusai, but I have been invited, and I think I may go, for Venice if not the conference.

I hope that your books have been coming along well. How exciting to have received that offer from the English publisher! Just when I was about to conclude that it is the fate of all good books to be neglected, I heard of this deserved recognition!

As ever, Donald

NAPLES, OCTOBER 17, 1999

Dear Donald—

I don't know why I shd take up the first half of this letter enumerating for you the thousand impediments that prevented my writing it long ago. They are all the usual things that New Yorkers, and travellers, are accustomed to, compounded by my dilatoriness—well, not really that, but it must look like dilatoriness to my wronged, and illustrious, correspondents. I loved having your letter, and the impression of your sea voyage, which roused strong memories. I've probably told you that, the first time I left Australia, just after the war, to go with my parents and sister to the east, the little ship, the Taiping (very comfortable, with at least two Chinese servants to every passenger) went from Sydney to Kure in five weeks, with only one stop—of a single afternoon, in New Guinea to take on water—and it didn't seem in the least long and the thrill of arriving, in a Red Dawn, at the top of the world, having started from the bottom . . . There had been no other way for Australians (or almost anyone) to travel outside their own country other than by ship, before the war; and during the war only combatants were travelling by air. Sea travel went on well into the 1950s as an unchallenged means of moving around the world. Jet planes put an end to it, of course. One of the marvellous aspects is, or was, being free from interruptions: "they can't get at me". But I suppose all that is changed, and your fellow passengers were often babbling into cellular phones? Spirits <u>can</u> cross water, these days. Having said that, I realise that we are entering, here, the season when Capri is cut off from the mainland quite regularly by high seas, sometimes for a couple of days: a pleasant and exclusive feeling.

[. . .]

I went for nearly a month to England and Scotland, seeing the English publishers, and staying with a series of dear and kind friends who cut a wide swath between Dorset and the Hebrides. What wonderful things I have seen. Have you ever been to the island of Staffa? (Mendelssohn, Hebrides Overture, Fingal's Cave, etc?) During those weeks, I went to the country house (divine, in Buckinghamshire) of an old friend, David Sainsbury, whom I first knew when he was twenty and who is now sixty, a lord, and a cabinet minister (for the sciences). To my surprise, he reminded me that I had told him, when he was on a trip to NYC in recent years, and we were speaking of Japan, of the immortal—truly—evening of your apotheosis at Columbia, and of how one of your former prisoners of war had spoken of your original meeting with him on Okinawa. David has said that in this way—my having spoken of the ceremony and you—he had become aware of your works and was "trying to get you" for a conference in the autumn in Britain. Do you recognise this conference? If you do meet David, you will find an original, thoughtful man phenomenally unimpressed by having been born into wealth and power, and entirely free from the British class affliction.

As to conferences—If you are coming to Venice, can you drop in at Naples? I could not promise to retain the run of glorious weather we have now had ever since I arrived in mid-September; but at present the little sun-trap of the Marina Piccola on Capri is thick with swimmers, the island is in its autumn reflowering—full of roses and jasmine and plumbago, and empty of boutiques and tourists (not quite empty, but a great diminution): a paradise. [. . .] I think you haven't seen Naples since so many monuments and museums have been beautifully restored—a surprise. And much is open to the public that was closed and derelict before. On Capri, my little "casa" is a great success to me, like living up in the sky on a blue and white tiled shelf. [. . .]

I was honoured to think that I could figure in one of your dreams, even while haranguing you to go to Reggio Emilia. I think we had better go there, since you have introduced the idea, as I've never seen it and it is packed with works of art—a famous Duomo, churches, what one can in Italy off-handedly refer to as "the usual". What a wonderful country it still is. Arriving in September, I stayed three days with beloved friends in Milan—one of the sons of the family in whose house I lived long ago at Siena. [. . .] They took me to see the restored Last Supper. I am too ignorant to speak of it in any detail, but the entire work seemed far more alive to me this time, and not merely for its colouring. I know that Everett (Fahy) has some reservations, but he thought that nothing better could have been done. (He also said, since it has been in a state of ruin for centuries, and badly damaged in the war, that it was either a choice of doing what they could with new techniques or of letting the entire work decay conclusively (the latter being what Everett calls "the Christian Science approach to art restoration")). I found it rather thrilling. That church is very beautiful—another heroic feat of rescue, after dreadful bombardment in the war. My friends live in the very centre of Milan, in a delightful apartment in a tree-lined street off Via Manzoni, and I walked a good bit around those familiar places, so sophisticated after Naples; and went to the beautiful Poldi-Pezzoli. [. . .]

I think this letter is now a dismaying length—the length that causes the reader to groan aloud on opening the envelope. However, I keep wondering how the last Meiji is revealing himself, and whether—in your customary prolific way—you have come near the end of his story? That, too, I'd be glad to hear about when you reach Italy and Venice. November can be very nice in Venice—weather chancy but not always cold, and with the Piazza empty in the evenings when the tourists have all gone off in their motorised gondolas to their mainland hotels.

In a few days, the 20th, Francis will have been dead five years. It is terrible to me to think and write that, and I must find some way to pass the day that would not have made him feel sad.

Here is a little fact that would not have been of interest to Ivan: there is a brief scene in War and Peace in which Cherubini's opera Les Deux Journées (The Water-Carrier) is mentioned; but since that opera is from 1804, it fails to scramble into Ivan's classification of 18th century acceptables. (The scene is when Natasha takes up her guitar—during the months in which Prince Andre has fatally left her alone in Russia while he goes abroad—and sings to it the air from the chorus. She had been to hear the opera in Saint Petersburg with Prince A.)

[. . .]

As to World News, how can one dwell on it? I will only mention that the Vesuvius has rumbled and caused tremors during the past week. I can't remember if Fujiyama is active and has a plume of smoke? I do know that it gives good luck to travellers when it becomes visible at the time of departure . . . I think we've been lucky—so far—in our relations with our respective volcanoes.

I'll be one among the many glad to see you again, whether in New York or in Italy. I wonder where you will be put up in Venice? I was there last year—it is really visibly imperilled, which makes one want to get there all the more. Perhaps next year . . .

With all affection, dear Donald, from Shirley

TOKYO, NOVEMBER 5, 1999

Dear Shirley,

I was very pleased indeed to receive your letter.

[. . .]

It is amazing that you should have written about David Sainsbury. Yesterday I got a letter from the Sainsbury Institute to give a lecture in June and today I answered that I would be delighted. The Foundation is also planning to collaborate with the center at Columbia founded in my name. Your letter makes me sure that I shall like him. Yesterday (memorable day!) I also received an honorary doctorate from the Tokyo University of Foreign Languages. At the reception afterwards I met the Director of the School of Oriental and African Languages at the University of London. I thought what I would have given earlier in my career to work under such a man. I was also greatly pleased that three former students of mine are teaching at the School. I may develop into a Mr. Chips after all.

Your mention of the scene in <u>War and Peace</u> in which Cherubini's opera is mentioned made me want, quite suddenly, to read the book again. Yesterday (what a busy day it was!) I had the recollection I always have of Anna Karenina while waiting alone on a train platform. I can't explain why, but I have reread Dostoevski novels but not Tolstoi's, no doubt because I <u>think</u> I remember them well . . . Or perhaps I fear they won't be as magnificent as I remember them. I sometimes have that experience. There is an Indian film called <u>The Music Room</u> about a maharajah who has a castle on a lonely shore. I saw it a long time ago and over the years it had built up in my memory as the perfect evocation of the power of music. Then I saw it again last year and was deeply disappointed. I had somehow contrived to blot out all the details that disappointed me on second viewing, leaving only the wind-swept shore, the disintegrating palace, and the maharajah who uses all his remaining money for a final concert.

I am nearing the completion of my account of Emperor Meiji. Because it is being serialized in Japanese, I have had to plan each episode independently, with a suitable ending for each. Now I shall have to break down the sixty-odd units to make them fit within the covers of a single book. I shall also have to decide just how much historical information that does not directly relate to Meiji should be included. I am afraid that I have not yet "found" Meiji and probably never will, and this may disappoint readers.

To answer your question: Fuji has not been active since the 9th century. This is a useful piece of information for scholars of literature: if a poem mentions the plume of smoke it must have been written before the last eruption. I have recently been in Kagoshima where my hotel room faced directly an active volcano called Sakurajima. It made a marvelous sight, especially at sunset.

[. . .]

As always, Donald

POSTCARD, NORWICH, JUNE 3, 2000

Dear Shirley,

Last night I delivered my talk in Norwich at the magnificent cathedral. Apparently I read my manuscript in an intelligible manner, but I was so tired that I had no recollection of what I had read. All in all, however, it was an unforgettable experience. I am thankful that I have lived to be 78 (this month). I love England, especially Norwich!

I met your friends the Sainsbury's and we talked of you with great affection.

As ever, Donald

TOKYO, JUNE 19, 2000

Dear Shirley,

I feel rather embarrassed when I recall the somewhat excessively euphoric postcard I sent you from Norwich. I hope that I did not seem too pleased with myself. It <u>was</u> an unforgettable experience, and I thought I should tell you about it. After Norwich I had two delightful days in Cambridge [. . .], beautiful as always. The only new thing was the admission charged to tourists by each of the colleges. I suppose they need the funds, but I felt nostalgic for the old days when the colleges could assume that no one who didn't belong there would intrude.

From London I flew to Luxembourg. I believe I had told you of my great "fan" in Luxembourg. He is a professor of Greek and Sanskrit but has taught himself to read Japanese. He and his delightful wife showed me much of the country. It is small but varied and the villages seem like those I imagine existed throughout Europe before 1914. The people at home speak Luxemburgish, which is about as far from German as Dutch is, but they are all required to learn both French and German from their early schooling. The newspapers have articles in both languages, seemingly unrelated to the content; they assume that the readers can read both French and German without difficulty. The street signs are all in French and the food is definitely French, but the people all have German surnames. A delightful place.

[. . .]

Now I am back in Tokyo. Yesterday I had my 78th birthday. It seems incredible. Am I really that old? So many of my friends here have died. In fact, when I have a telephone call I can be pretty sure that it is a business call—someone who wants me to give a lecture or write an article. I keep debating whether I should reverse the part of the year I spend here (two-thirds) and the part I spend in New York (the rest). One reason for staying here, I now realize though I had not been aware of this before, is that there are people who to some degree depend on my being here. Probably I will enjoy my life here more once I begin some major project. I am thinking of writing a biography of a fifteenth-century shogun. It will be difficult, I know, but I so much enjoyed writing my biography of Emperor Meiji.

[. . .]

I am enclosing an article about Cesare Valetti. I met him twice in New York, but I know that you were a friend, and his death must come as a loss. I remember him especially for his appearances in the Mozart operas. What a beautiful voice he had!

[. . .]

Best wishes as always, yours, Donald

I am reading The Way We Live Now by Trollope, an extraordinary novel. I hope this does not set me off on a Trollope binge—I must do other work!

TOKYO, JULY 18, 2000

Dear Shirley,

I was so pleased to talk with you when you telephoned. There are so many things that have gone wrong with the world, even during the past thirty years, that it is agreeable to think of something which has improved—telephone service. When I first lived in Kyoto it took about two hours to get through to Tokyo, let alone any more distant place. My recollections of international calls at that time are mainly of fear that I would dial a wrong number and then, at some vast cost, have to try again. [. . .] And now it is all so simple. Too simple perhaps. Receiving a letter has become a much more unusual pleasure.

[. . .]

At the moment I am translating a short novel about the Japanese defense of an island (Peleliu) in the South Pacific in 1944.[1] The author evidently studied documents of the period carefully and there is a kind of authenticity that impresses me. There is an antithesis between the Japanese sergeant who stands for the samurai virtues and a Korean corporal who is desperately eager to be accepted by the Japanese but cannot go along with the rigid fanaticism of the sergeant. The author is someone I first met forty years ago when he was about to go to Harvard to study classical Greek. He later became involved in politics, especially during the Vietnam War, when he organized a group which encouraged American sailors to desert and spirited them off to Sweden. He has more recently become involved with Korea. His wife is Korean and he has written about his experiences with his wife's family. (This probably accounts for the Korean corporal.) The book is certainly not what one would expect someone with his background to write, but I do not think it represents a rejection of his iconoclastic attitudes. In reading the book one may feel sorry for the Japanese on the island, bombed and strafed by innumerable American planes, but I don't think anyone would wish that the Japanese had won. (A footnote: after all these years, the author <u>has</u> gone back to the classics. He has published a Japanese translation of Longinus on the sublime.)

My life in Tokyo is rather dull, partly because it is so hot that I don't feel like going anywhere. I am not precisely lonely, but I realize as I write this letter that I have nothing very exciting to report. I can never seem to make up my mind whether I prefer to spend a day entirely in this apartment, engaged in translation, or whether I really would like to have dinner with some delightful people. Probably I shall never know!

My bedtime reading is <u>Mary Barton</u> by Mrs. Gaskell. I picked up the book at an outdoor stall, thinking that all I knew of her writings was <u>Cranford</u>, and I had largely forgotten that. It is not a very good novel, but it provides a marvelous evocation of the grim life of the lower classes in Manchester in the 1830s. I am sure you know it—like every other book!

[. . .]

All my best wishes.
As ever, Donald

TOKYO, NOVEMBER 26, 2000

Dear Shirley,

It was a great relief and joy to have your telephone call. Although I told myself that the reason why I had not heard from you was that you were too occupied with your novel to write anything else, I couldn't quite put from my mind the possibility that you might be ill. And indeed, though it proved to be a false scare, you yourself probably thought that you were seriously ill. My intuition was partly correct, but I wish that it had been totally incorrect and that you had been happily writing your book all that time.

I have begun work on my biography of the shogun Ashikaga Yoshimasa.[2] He is a strange figure—an ineffectual though not wicked ruler, a man so dominated by his wife that he has been held up to ridicule by Japanese historians, a military man who during a war that lasted ten years and resulted in the almost entire destruction of the city of Kyoto refused to have anything to do with the fighting. He would not be remembered today were it not for the fact that the arts he fostered—gardens, tea ceremony, ink painting and so on—have emerged as the most typical Japanese arts. When Japanese speak (as they often do) of the "Japanese soul" or something similar, they usually refer to arts that developed during Yoshimasa's reign which have since acquired a special aura. I know that wicked monarchs have been great patrons of the arts, but I haven't found other examples of a ruler who was a fiasco in his appointed duties but who largely contributed to the formation of the culture of his country.

[. . .]

I have been disappointed that my agent Georges Borchardt has not yet been able to place the short novel about the Japanese defense of an island in the South Pacific. Perhaps nobody wants to read about those long-ago events, especially when (in Borchardt's words) the Americans are portrayed as demons. No doubt some day he'll find an interested university press, but even if he doesn't, it will not be a great tragedy for me. I think, however, that like it or not it is worth knowing how a Japanese writer of prevailingly left-wing views recalls the militarism of the past.

I hear absolutely nothing from New York. [. . .] I had planned to return to New York early in January, but was invited to the first poetry reading of the year, held in the presence of the emperor and empress. I had been invited before, but always at a time when I couldn't go, so I accepted. I am sure that it will not be anything extraordinary, but I like old rituals, and I look forward to hearing the poems composed by members of the Imperial Family sung to the same tune that has been used for many centuries.

I hope that all goes well with you and your work after the shock of the doctor's false report. I truly look forward to seeing you again in January. I return on the 16th.

As ever, Donald

CAPRI, DECEMBER 6, 2000

Dear Donald—

About six years ago I learned that this blue paper, on which I've written to friends now for forty years and which came from Pineider in Florence, was being axed (being "discontinued", as "They" now say).

A friend at Florence hightailed it to Pineider in Via Tornabuoni on my behalf, and I duly received a large quantity of pads and envelopes—boxes thereof. It would seem odd to you, who know me as the world's worst correspondent, to learn that this immense quantity is now dwindling, and that I rummage around for a last few sheets of this or that size, or an airmail envelope of the old blue. (Pineider meanwhile has branched out into expensive tooled leather "items" of note cases, desk sets, and so on, letting essentials go to the wall.) Perhaps we may live to see writing-paper itself become obsolete—and of course the typewriter. The typewriter on which I'm at present pounding was given to me forty years ago when I first began to write for publication. Much of my work, such as it is, was produced on it—it started out pale green, but has grown grey in my service.

Thank you so much—well for everything; most of all for your forbearing friendship. The Maxwells died, virtually together, in late July. I am so grateful for your thought of me—yes, an extraordinary writer and man. Emmy died of the cancer she had been drastically treated for during almost two years. She had stayed because of Bill, otherwise wd not have gone through with a "cure" that ultimately had its role in her death. In the end, he stayed for her. When she died he took to his bed, stopped eating (he was already thin as a cobweb), and died one week later. A distinguished and in its way beautiful departure, both of them utterly lucid and alert to the last, attended by close friends to whom they had wanted to say goodbye. Four days before Emmy's death, preparations were made for them both to go in wheelchairs to the Chardin exhibition, which they had passionately wanted to see. Bill got up several times from his chair to look into the paintings closely; Emmy was happy, and came home exhausted. Isn't there something of the ancient world in this?—Socrates wanting to learn to play the lyre on the eve of his death, the gathering of friends in an acknowledged occasion of departure. There was a memorial ceremony after Labour Day at Saint John the Divine, various friends spoke. Such private people they were, Emmy and Bill; yet that huge place was packed to the doors. I don't know how many were there—I'm not good at such guesses—but certainly a thousand. Magnificent day, slightly autumnal, and there was a gathering afterwards in the church garden, where I had never before been and which has wonderful trees. Another great friend, the physicist Abraham Pais, died the same week in Copenhagen, suddenly: such a splendid and delightful man. As you say, these are not only regretted farewells, but there is the irrefutable sense of dwindling: humanism itself on the way out. What Yeats wrote in his late years:

And I am in despair that Time may bring
Approved patterns of women and of men,
But not that self-same excellence again.

Excellence itself is not a word one can expect to hear common now, very often—unless for advertising a car or a kitchen cleanser.

There will be the memorial for Bill at the Academy in April. It was decided not to give it in November since there were "already six lined up" (our thinning ranks . . .), and it was felt that Bill shd have some particular attention. Updike suggested that I should give the talk, which I'm honoured to do, though who can be worthy of such a figure? (Updike himself wrote a piece, quite good and with more heart than one might have expected, that was published in The New Yorker.)

[. . .]

Now, for allegría. I look forward intensely to your January return. Alas, I think I won't be back in time for the Academy members' dinner, which is I think on the 17th of January? I hope you can come to dinner almost immediately thereafter? Of course I wonder about publication of the translation of the Palau novel, when will that be? There is much more curiosity about the Japanese experience of the war, now—I need hardly tell you—among Americans, but such a poor quality of history in English, I think [. . .]. I'm enclosing, among other clippings, a review of a book on Hirohito that has been much praised. [. . .]. No doubt you know the book, and perhaps also its author Mr. Bix? And I wonder what you think of it? No one in the USA ever seems aware of the British in Burma, the Australians in New Guinea and the islands, even the thousands of prisoners seized by the Japanese at the fall of Singapore and Malaya. On the plane coming from New York to Rome last month, a recent film ("the film") was shown of the epic of a submarine that, in 1943, managed, thanks to the USA and the US Navy, to capture the Enigma code. What can the reception of such a farce have been in Britain, or in Poland? Something beyond xenophobia, the USA seems in its total power these days to have lost curiosity, imagination, inquiry into the immediate past of the rest of the world.

[. . .] I am here on Capri closing up—in a continuity of such glorious weather that it seems madness to go. Yet I'll be glad to open my NYC door again, and to see my friends. The island is silent, unvisited—many people would think melancholy at evening— divine. Of course there will soon be storms, lower temperatures, rain.

But these extraordinary days can't be taken from us. Something strikes me now, about my Capri part-time existence of forty-three years now—that, when I first knew the island in the 1950s and was in my twenties, and for many years thereafter, I was aware of a number of foreigners living on the island—not a "colony", all singular persons, or in couples—people of various nationalities, French, British, Scandinavian, German, who had obviously loved Capri for many years, known it between the wars or even earlier, and had made it their home or part-time home. These were reflective, civilised personalities, some of them writers or artists, no air of celebrity or exclusiveness, or even of pronounced eccentricity; but distinctive, and often with an unostentatious "style" of their own, and individual manner of dressing that might be outdated in a pleasant way and was always simple and appropriate. One imagined that such elders would always exist. Well, I now realise that I am probably the last of the tribe. I felt at home with their existence, and I suppose it's now the existence I perpetuate, without thinking of it. Foreigners who now come for any length of time to the island are not, so far as I'm aware, of the genre. Indeed, the genre, having lasted a long time, is probably now extinct. It was scattered through the world—in Egypt, in Persia, the Indies, Sicily, possibly in Latin America. Not bohemian, not gypsy-like, not Taos or Oaxaca. You will know what I mean.

Of course I wonder now what is happening with your Meiji book, and what will be—perhaps already is—your next theme. How wonderful that you quietly, I'd say reclusively almost, do this momentous exigent work, complete your book, and choose the next one. Fortunate Japan, in having Keene-san in its history. [. . .]

Speaking of extinction, do you know that wonderful story by Tomasi di Lampedusa (author of The Gattopardo), diversely called in English either Professor and the Mermaid, or The Siren, or Lighea? I think it one of the loveliest things written in the second half of the troubled 20th century, and—if you don't know it—shall be privileged to press a copy on you when you return. That will be next month—2001, incredibly. Much, then, to catch up on. Of course I hope that the coming year will bring a slight change at least in your itinerary so that you will be more in New York and/or Italy. Let us see. Meantime, I wish you every good, dear Donald, and will be so happy to see you again.

Shirley
At the time of your return there will be a presidential inauguration—of whom? How <u>awful</u> is this Bush.

TOKYO, DECEMBER 17, 2000

Dear Shirley,

Today the postman brought an envelope covered with beautiful Italian stamps. I have never received such a splendid envelope before.

[. . .]

I share your apprehensions about Bush. He will be like his father, a tool in the hands of the big industrialists, who say, "God Bless America!" even as they fire half of their employees. He isn't much to come home to, but the Prime Minister here in Japan is just as bad.

[. . .]

My biography of Emperor Meiji seems to be moving along slowly but surely at Columbia University Press. At least I have the feeling they really want to want to publish the book. Oddly enough, the publication of the Japanese translation seems stalled, though there is at least a chance that it will do well. But I am not worried. Georges Borchardt informs me that both Knopf and Grove have turned down my translation of the novel about Palau [. . .].

I am reading <u>Madame Bovary</u> again. What a book! I don't know the book by Tomasi de Lampedusa, but I will, when I return. All my best wishes for Christmas and the New Year—as ever, Donald

TOKYO, JUNE 17, 2001

Dear Shirley,

I have been meaning to write you for so long that I feel as if I have already written. I wanted most of all to tell you what a delightful stay I had in Denmark thanks to Ida Nicolaisen. The night at your house when you seated us together at table we had a most pleasant conversation during the course of which I mentioned that I was going to Sweden to give some lectures. She said that she would be happy if I went on to Copenhagen, and that is what came about. She is so warm and simpatica that I feel as if I have known her most of my life.

Stockholm was beautiful but cold. I had looked in the New York Times each day for the temperature in Stockholm, and concluding that it was probably much the same as New York, I did not take any warm clothes. I learned after arrival that the week during which I had examined the temperature was a freak occurrence, a week of summer sandwiched in between layers of normal winter weather. Copenhagen was much warmer and everything went extremely well.

I had two days in Berlin, the first time I have visited that city since I was taken there by my father when I was nine. I recalled absolutely nothing of my first visit. People had told me what an exciting city it is, and probably they have good reason for saying so, but I did not like it, no doubt because it was in sharp contrast to my visits to Stockholm and Copenhagen where I had friends. Also, everybody I met there spoke English, and in Berlin where I knew nobody and cannot speak German, I was no more than a tourist. There are several fine museums and, best of all, I went to Potsdam which is much more in my style.

I have been back in Tokyo for over two weeks. I was afraid that I would feel lonely now that all my closest friends are dead, but I have been kept so busy that I have little time for brooding. I shall go to Okinawa later this week. An imaginative television producer has decided to do a long program on Japanese prisoners of war who were captured on Okinawa in 1945. I seem to be one of the few language officers left to tell the story, and I have already spent several afternoons talking to widows and children of prisoners. I find it surprising that I remember anything after fifty-odd years, but the young producer presses me for details and cannot understand why I am not more precise.

I am reading War and Peace. Do you remember asking me when I first read it? I was fifteen then. I read it again during the war, but have not looked at it since. When I heard that Bill Maxwell asked to have it read to him as he was dying, I thought I must read it again. I am about halfway through and already I am regretting that the book is not longer. I have recently had a bit to do with deconstructionists and the like. I find their theories not only unappealing but irrelevant, insofar as I can understand them. I have not read anything written by them concerning War and Peace and I shall not. It is overpowering in its truth. It needs no exegesis.

I have been fighting off engagements in August in the hope I can go to New York. I have not actually attempted to buy a ticket and it may be difficult at the height of the Japanese tourist season, but it would give me much pleasure to see you again.

I hope that your book is coming along well. My serial on Ashikaga Yoshimasa, a strange 15th century shogun, is proving to be more difficult to write than I had anticipated. The Japanese translation by Shiro of my book on Nō has been selling well for a book of that kind.

All my best wishes,
As ever, Donald

ROME, JULY 7, 2001

Dear Donald—

With what pleasure I received your letter, which had many revelations for me (including the existence of Ashikaga Yoshimara, of whose "strangeness" I hope to learn more from you); and which suggests that you may really come to New York in August. To speak ecstatically, that will make a luminous difference to my summer there—as well as to the city. And I try to will the event into reality . . .

You will remember, as I do, the nightmare NY summers of life before air conditioning. Of the stadium concerts masterminded by that valiant though rather amateurish old lady (probably younger then than I am now), and Dantesque subway temperatures. There is a story of JD Salinger's, "Raise High The Roofbeam, Carpenters", set in just such a NY summer in about 1942, that immortally gives the atmosphere. Well, I reluctantly concede that some details have got better.

[. . .]

What will your experience of Okinawa render, I wonder. Please forgive a banality, but surely this return, and the recall it must evoke, will become a book? The press is full here (in Italy, but also in Britain, and presumably more so in America) of Okinawa at present, with the US conceding the extradition of the American serviceman to the Japanese courts. Italians are particularly interested because the refusal of the United States to allow American offenders to be tried in Italy has been a big scandal here. US servicemen are then of course exonerated by their own military courts, the most flagrant injustice being the case of the pilots who, playing aerial games, snapped the cable of a ski lift in north Italy, causing many deaths, about two years ago.

[. . .]

Bill Maxwell's re-reading of War and Peace came about because he and I, in the spring of 2000, were among those asked to read aloud something of our choice at a little evening "benefit" for Ned O'Gorman's children's library in Harlem. Shortly before this was to happen, I was having tea at the Maxwells' and Bill asked me what I was going to read. I said, a poem about Verona by a "1940s" English poet; and a passage from War and Peace. Emmy went to the bookshelves to bring W & P so that I could show them the passage (it is the immortal page or two in which Prince Andrei leaves his army on the blistering march to the battle of Borodino and turns off into his own abandoned property, where he is briefly restored to humanity and dailiness, and where two bare legged little girls are taking plums from the overgrown orchard. It is perfect. Emmy then discovered that their W & P was not on the shelves but at their country place. The next morning I delivered to their place a copy of the Rosemary Edmonds' translation (by far the best in English, I think) in heavy Penguin; and Bill began to read it. He told me, "It is so comforting"— in their mortal circumstances, then. That was in March. By late May the book became too heavy for him to hold; and Annabel came each afternoon to read it to him. He finished it on a Saturday almost a year ago, in late July. Emmy died on the following Monday, and Bill one week later. Now, the anniversary.

Sometimes he and I would go over a scene he had just read— not, oh God, "discussing" it, still less "interpreting" it, but giving the homage of our pleasure in it. When we spoke about the scene in which Nicolas Rostov tells his father that he has lost a fortune at gambling—a fortune that the Rostovs don't have—we both wept, for the beauty of it.

I too first read W & P in adolescence. I was sixteen and living in Hong Kong with my parents, and deeply in love with a White Russian who had much of the character of Prince Andrei. Then, of course, I did not give great attention to Tolstoy's great disquisitions on war, which now I know well and find full of wisdom. Extraordinary that L.T. could, among so much else, write with absolute authority on "strategy" and battle, and life under arms—having lived that life also. The epilogue, where he turns Natasha into a fat frump, is hateful to me, apart from one or two details. In something of the same way, I think, he later set up the beauty and character of Anna Karenina and then destroyed her into a neurotic shrew. However, fortunately, he could not "destroy" either of his immortal heroines.

I've never been to Germany—just because it hasn't happened. I imagine Potsdam wd be more "à mon rayon", too, than Berlin.

Of this, too, I'd like to hear more in August. Stockholm was beautiful, the only time we were there; it was August, which no doubt helped, because I wd dread the long lightless winter. Your lack of warm clothes recalled to me the awful account in yr "memoires" of being in Alaskan regions without—for petty bureaucratic reasons—warm uniforms, in 1942 . . .

As you see, I'm in Rome, en route to New York. Much to say of a beautiful Italian stay. Yes, thank you, I've done much work. Rome never loses its excitement. Splendour. How I miss Francis here. With all affection, dear Donald, and hoping intensely for a reunion in August—Shirley

USAMI, SEPTEMBER 8, 2001

Dear Shirley,

I'm now in my little place on the coast of Izu, about an hour and half away from Tokyo. I have just one room in what the Japanese call a "resort mansion," but I can see the sea, & that is important. It does <u>not</u> rival the sea either at Naples or Capri, but it is good to get away from the incessant demands made of me in Tokyo, mainly by good people whom I like, but demands all the same—for a lecture, an article, an hour of my time. Sometimes I refuse, and then I receive such a piteous letter, so full of sadness, so clinging to the faint hope that I may relent, that of course I do. It is very flattering, but also depletes my energy and keeps me from doing what I want to do, such as writing to you.

[. . .]

The television broadcast which I did in July & which was shown on the 14th of August had great success. I have appeared on television many times, and have generally felt after the broadcast that it was a stupid waste of time. This time the subject was my relations with Japanese prisoners of war during the fighting on Okinawa. The great majority of Japanese today were born after the war and most have forgotten the ideology and even the events. I think that this program may have done some good, if only to remind Japanese of the war. Of course, they all know about the atomic bombs dropped on Hiroshima and Nagasaki, and every time an American soldier on Okinawa does anything wrong (a fairly common occurrence, unfortunately) it is prominently featured in the press. But they do not know how many Japanese, deceived by the propaganda of the Japanese military, leaped from cliffs to preserve their honor. The sight of the names of all who died in the battle for Okinawa, whether from enemy bullets or after pressing a hand grenade to the chest, is truly horrendous.

I have been writing with some difficulty a serial on the fifteenth-century shogun Yoshimasa. One problem is that I must produce a manuscript every month, whether or not moved by inspiration. I would like to do the whole thing over again, this time at my own pace.

I have had little time for reading, but every night I read a chapter or two of a novel by Trollope. I find his novels very uneven. The one I am reading now <u>He Knew He Was Right</u> has an extremely interesting central theme—a marriage wrecked by a jealous husband and a wife whose insistence on her independence takes a most trivial form—but the sub-plots are tedious. He probably was paid by the page. Other Trollope novels have interesting characters and sometimes the situations seem surprisingly contemporary, but he seems second-rate when compared to Dickens or to any of the great women novelists.

[. . .]

As ever, Donald

TOKYO, JULY 7, 2002

Dear Shirley,

It is hard to believe that over a month has passed since I saw you last. First came the trip to Ireland and Norway with one day in Edinburgh in between. I was fortunate in Ireland because acquaintances—the man, the former Irish ambassador to Japan—saw to it that every day was filled with agreeable things to do. I was happy to have been able to meet Seamus Heaney. I had in fact met him briefly at the Academy on some occasion, but this time we had a couple of hours together. I regret now that I wasn't able to do what you can do so effortlessly, recite my favorite poems of his. But perhaps the pervading genial atmosphere was not conducive to the recitation of his poems. I have read not only his poems but his criticism, especially "The Redress of Poetry" which I much admire.

I visited Trinity College and was impressed by the architecture, especially the wonderful library. Dinner at High Table, however, was something of a disappointment, mainly because I was surrounded by Mechanical Engineers and the like who were desperately trying to think of something to tell me about Japan.

Bergen is a lovely town. The houses are painted in bright colors, no doubt one way to cheer people during the long winters. The hotel was filled with Americans in wheelchairs. Some sort of conference or reunion, I suppose. It was easy to escape to the picturesque water-front and enjoy the distant snow-covered mountains.

This was my first visit to Edinburgh in over fifty years. In the winter of 1950, I think, I spent about a month there, taking advantage of the Christmas holiday at Cambridge. I chose Edinburgh because I had been told it was the cheapest place in Europe. It was bitterly cold, and the only heating in my room was an electric heater the size of a brick on which I rested first one hand and then the other. I managed to complete writing the revised edition of "The Japanese Discovery of Europe," but my most pervasive memory is of the cold and of the days that did not get bright until nine but were dark again by three. I went several times to the National Gallery, and went there again this time. The collection has become incomparably richer, and I enjoyed being in an old-fashioned museum with one picture above another. I remembered from my previous visit having seen wax models of sculpture by Michelangelo. I asked about them this time, but a very friendly lady could find no record of such objects. Perhaps it was not Michelangelo. You are the only person I know who might know.

[...]

I have nothing whatever to report about Tokyo. I have given two lectures and will give more before I leave, but I have not been able to do my own work.

All my best wishes, Donald

TOKYO, NOVEMBER 12, 2002

Dear Shirley,

It came as a shock to me this morning to realize that we have not been in touch since August. Unless one does something to make time stop passing the months disappear, rather in the way of old-fashioned Hollywood movies in which leaves dropped from a calendar to indicate the rapid passage of time.

My stay in Japan has been happy on the whole and even very happy in the last two or three weeks. I learned first of all that I had been named a Person of Cultural Merit, the title that sounds less silly in Japanese than in English. There was no statement informing me of why I had been chosen, but I suppose that it was because of my contributions to making Japanese culture better known abroad.

This is only the second time a non-Japanese has been recognized with this decoration. To my surprise I discovered that I will receive a monthly grant for the rest of my life. The sum is modest, but it is pleasant to think that I needn't worry about money.

The second good thing that happened was the award made by a Japanese newspaper to my book <u>Emperor of Japan</u> as the best work of nonfiction published in the preceding year. This, too, was most welcome, of course.

Last night I finished making corrections on the manuscript of my book on the creation of a new Japanese culture in the late 15th century. It will be published by Columbia University Press, presumably next year. The Japanese edition will appear in January. Today I am to meet an editor to discuss illustrations. I am always astonished by the rapidity with which the Japanese can produce a book. But, of course, they don't have to learn all twenty-six letters of the alphabet!

I hope that your work has progressed smoothly. Perhaps it will be completed by the time I return to New York, on the 9th of January.

As ever, Donald

NEW YORK, NOVEMBER 28, 2002

Now 7th Dec, Pearl Harbour Day . . .

Dear Donald—

I'd no sooner typed the above November date than the city dropped on me—"in they broke, those people of Importance": this, a quotation from Browning, from a marvellous poem about avocations of great artists. The particular theme in this case being a reference, in the Vita Nuova of Dante, to Dante's having started to paint an angel, when the servant (lucky Dante) came to tell him that "persons who could not be denied" wanted to see him. Of course, the angel evaporated. [. . .] I am also working, happily and passionately, on my novel, still hoping to give it to Jonathan Galassi in late February. I don't know whether I can do that, but it will be thereabouts.

I realised from your most welcome letter that you have finished your book on decoration and culture in the fifteenth century. How is this possible?—you seem such a decorous man, but there must be a thunderbolt within. One would think your <u>Emperor</u> might have served as laurels to rest on for a year or two at least (for anyone else, a life's work). I enclose the fine TLS review, which I'm sure you will have seen; but an extra copy never seems de trop. [. . .]

Your autumn in Japan has been, I see, triumphant. All your admirers and friends throughout the world have known you to be a Person of Cultural Merit; but it's delightful and heartening to learn that you've been so recognised formally in Japan, and that bounty is attached to the title. I have a glimmer of an idea what the ceremonies must be like in connection with such an honour, compounded—if that's the word—by the award for best nonfiction for your Emperor. I remember that you've had similar recognition in Japan before. I suppose that a different culture from America's would celebrate these distinctions at home on your behalf, and be proud. But this kind of acknowledgement tends, in America, to fall to a rock star or sportsman. I came back from Italy a month ago to attend the board meeting at the Academy, arriving a little early—on 5 November—in order to vote in the half-term elections, the polls closing early that evening. Next morning I woke to calamitous results—the entire country going to the Republicans, it seemed—and felt like bolting back to Rome. Already the victors are seizing the spoils, with drastic effects on the judiciary, the forests, the Alaska wilderness; with flagrant pay offs to Bush supporters, every evil one can think of. A "home security" bill has been pushed through, which will mean that every invasion of privacy can be inflicted on us without our right of appeal.

Meantime, the obsession with making war intensifies, and the world seems to be in flames. Forgive these thoughts, which are only what we all know. The arts, the libraries and museums, the ever precarious culture of this paradoxical country—these count for nothing as far as the administration and a large part of the electorate are concerned; or there is outright hostility to them. How long and hard has been the creation of civilised institutions and private thoughtfulness, creativity, decency; and how brutally and quickly swept away in this most powerful country.

Better things—that you will be here on 9 January. We'll rejoice, if you'll allow. Ida Nicolaisen comes back at the same time, with high hopes of seeing you. She was here briefly in November, and we dined together. As we walked along in the early dark to L'Absinthe, where we paused at the very spot where the three of us laughed so delightedly about your encounter on top of the Mayan pyramid; and we laughed all over again. (Do you remember that a man passing, with two or three companions, turned with a smile and said to us, "I wish I knew what it was.")

[...]

I wish I had met Seamus Heaney when he came to the Academy—I think I was away. I admire his poetry and his writings on poetry very much, and his "persona", which has always been without self-importance and uncompromised in intelligence and feeling. I was, in a minor way, troubled by his recent insistence that poetry can now only be important when it comes from persons and cultures which/who have suffered from, for instance, totalitarianism and persecution—eg Eastern Europe. He is greatly impressed by the Eastern European poets, who often indeed seem profound and beautiful; and says—this is trickier—that he feels confident that he understands them fully from translations. I don't care for this concept of "significance" in poetry. Auden's insistence that "poetry makes nothing happen" goes—though I understand his cautionary feeling and sympathise with it—too far, I feel, since one cannot guarantee that poetry makes nothing happen, ie, is never "publicly" beneficial. But I am infinitely closer to that point of view than to Heaney's rather newly propounded one. English poetry has rarely sprung from persons publicly afflicted—where would Thomas Hardy be in a stricture of the kind, for instance? I think that Heaney would respond that our (terrifying) era calls for different qualities. Well, "our poetry" is lacking, mostly, in greatness at present. Literature, language, expression, writing itself—seemed to be deteriorating in the machine and electronic world. That doesn't mean that nothing more can happen for the better, or that only dire experiences can inspire.

When we were in Sweden, long ago, and hoping to go to Norway, I wanted to see Bergen, having once had a friend who came from there and who praised it. [. . .] Now I learn from you that it is a painted town, a sort of Pompeiian red and ochre and blue city. I don't see Edinburgh following suit. The gallery has been greatly improved by the present director (Clifford) whom I know quite well (they often come to NY, raising funds from rich people . . .). He has a genius for collecting funds and for spotting "blockbuster" paintings and drawings in obscure places—and acquiring them. As to the wax models—I will ask Everett Fahy, who goes to Edinburgh regularly, and who will certainly know about anything of the Renaissance kind. (Here I am replying to your lovely letter of last July, antedating your New York trip—I found the letter only on my return to Italy, after seeing you.) My autumn stay in Italy was celestial—for the most part, radiant weather, such light, and, on Capri, such serenity. I did a lot of work, which I continue here. New York makes its demands, however, especially at this Christmas season—in which our president urges us to "buy as much as possible", while every day the newspaper announces thousands of dismissals from factories and businesses . . . Did you see that a forthright Canadian official, a woman, called Bush an "imbecile", and had to resign.

I think I'll send her a congratulatory post card—of which I daresay she has many.

As to my work—you ask if it goes "smoothly". That is not the word, though I'm so happy doing it. It draws in part on experiences from my eastern youth, which I revisit with enchantment and anguish; and has involved the rereading, after many years, of diaries and letters that wring the heart. However, such things are usually fertile in one's work, and I hope that will be the case. And in fiction one can correct an ultimate tragedy into a suggestion, at least, of our "happy ending". That is, set Life right, as one can't manage to do in reality.

This will wish you, dear Donald, a joyful Christmas and New Year, and a triumphant start to the imponderable 2003. I can't tell you how I look forward to seeing you in a month from now. Shirley

TOKYO, AUGUST 5, 2003

Dear Shirley,

I feel terribly ashamed of myself when I realize I have not written since having your welcome telephone call. There has been no real reason. My time has been chopped up into oddly shaped segments, but there was nothing to prevent myself from calling a halt to my perpetual search for mislaid things, my chief occupation, at least long enough to write a letter.

July was rainy and delightfully cool. August has begun with a heat wave, so not as bad as the one afflicting Europe this year. I have had to go to Osaka three times and still have one more lecture there, in September. The trip, in an extremely fast and comfortable train, takes only a little over two hours, as opposed to seven and a half hours in 1955, but it is fatiguing all the same, and each year I make a futile vow not to do any more lecturing. The three lectures I gave in July were not my best, but the standard in Japan is rather low, and that makes my lectures seem better than they are. Or perhaps the standard is low everywhere; I managed to avoid attending lectures except if I know in advance they will be outstanding, like yours.

I have not been reading much. I'm slowly but surely making my way through an 800 page history of Mexico during the last 150 years. It is actually a very good history (by a man named Krauze, not very Mexican), and I'm enjoying it, though I suppose the main reason for having reached page 605 is that I feel ashamed of having known so little about a country I have several times visited. My knowledge of Mexican history came mainly from the films—Bette Davis as the unfortunate Carlota, Paul Muni as Juarez, and Wallace Beery as Pancho Villa. My only Mexican friend, Octavio Paz, was the most remarkable man, a true cosmopolite who was at the same time very Mexican. Last year I took part in a kind of symposium here in Tokyo at which Enrico Krause, a Japanese diplomat, and myself took turns talking about Octavio. It was very moving to me and, I think, to the audience.

Today I started writing my next book, on a nineteenth-century painter named Kazan.[3] I have been reading about him for about six months without writing a word (except notes), mainly because I haven't been able to decide the form in which the book should be cast. An even more important problem is that Kazan has been so exhaustively studied by Japanese scholars that I have searched in vain for something they have overlooked. Is it enough to present in English material already known to scholars of Japan? I haven't made up my mind, but I know that I must give three lectures in England in November about Kazan so I am disregarding for the moment questions of form and originality. But they will return if I really go through with publishing a whole book about him.

I suppose your book must be printed by now and possibly page proofs have been sent to reviewers. Naturally, I am excited at the prospect of this new book, especially because it will be at least in part about Japan. If you tell me the exact hour of publication I shall drink a glass of champagne to you!

[. . .]

As ever, Donald

Have you heard anything recently about Bill Weaver's condition? If he is able to read a letter I would like to write to him.

TOKYO, SEPTEMBER 29, 2003

Dear Shirley,

I returned this evening from a less than thrilling session at which a poet and I decided on who would receive a prize for a short essay in the mood of Bashō's <u>Narrow Road of Oku</u>, to find a copy of <u>The Great Fire</u>. I opened it with excitement. It looks beautiful. You had showed me the Turner painting that would be the cover, but I had not realized quite how beautiful it would look. Congratulations on what is destined to be another wonderful gift from you to the world—and especially to me.

[. . .]

My time in Japan has been cut up into not altogether satisfactory segments—lectures at many places, "dialogues", reading of entries submitted to contests (like the one today) and many meetings with people who want me to do something. I have written the three lectures I will give in England in November, my one achievement. It may be possible to judge from the reactions to the lectures whether or not I should attempt to write a whole book on the painter (19th century) I have been studying. There is certainly enough interesting material for three lectures, but perhaps that is all. In other words, I may have chosen a topic badly. I hope not!

I'm sorry now I did not go to New York in the summer, but at that time my work seemed to be going well and I rather dreaded the two long flights. But this year I have suddenly become aware that I am eighty-one. I don't mean that I am in failing health or that I have lost my memory. I have become conscious that there is a limit to what I can do, that the next may be my last book. I do not feel gloomy about this self-evident truth that I have managed to ignore, but I feel I must take advantage of the remaining time to see my friends as often as possible, to listen to as much music as possible, to read again the books that mean most to me.

[. . .]

Next week I shall give a talk to the Verdi society in Japan. Yes, there is one. I think I shall lecture on <u>Don Carlos</u>, not the best of Verdi's operas perhaps, but the one I always want to see or to listen to on records.

I hope that you are well, dear Shirley, and I look forward very much to seeing you on my return. As always, Donald

ASUKA, JULY 2, 2004

Dear Shirley,

I am now on a Japanese cruise ship that is travelling through fog on its way to Kamchatka by way of the Aleutian Islands. The fog no doubt will prevent me from experiencing nostalgia as we pass islands where, sixty-one years ago, I spent several miserable months. It is curious how well I remember things that happened, people I knew even slightly, though I probably would have difficulty remembering what I did six months ago . . .

I have been trying to study, but my eyes become very fatigued after an hour reading the small print of a Japanese book. Fortunately,

I brought with me a few books in English, which are not so difficult to read. I'm now about halfway through <u>The Rings of Saturn</u> by W G Sebald. No doubt you know this book, as you know everything worth reading, but I have been deeply moved by his descriptions of forgotten and crumbling places. The translation is a marvel. I would like the translator, Michael Hulse, to translate all of German literature! My German is very weak, useful only for factual material, and not of much use even then. Perhaps a translation of <u>Faust</u> by Michael Hulse would enable me to love a work that has never given me pleasure.

I thought of you just now because Sebald, after a brief but horrifying account of the massacre of Serbs in Croatia during the war passes on to a young officer, later distinguished as the secretary general of the United Nations. If by some chance you don't know <u>The Rings of Saturn</u>, I think you would find in Sebald a kindred spirit.

I have now been on the <u>Asuka</u> about two weeks. Most of the time was spent in Alaska, going from one small port to the next. The scenery is magnificent—great, snow-covered mountains and glaciers dripping into the sea. The towns look rather like Hollywood portrayals of the Wild West [. . .]. But one has only to look up, no matter in which direction, to see the mountains surrounding the prosaic little towns.

Those on the ship who have been to Kamchatka inform me that there is nothing to see, nothing to buy. I remember descriptions of Kamchatka from the eighteenth century when, we are told, the only commodity in abundance was vodka. I remember too what Chekhov wrote about his visit. I won't be disappointed as long as Kamchatka is sufficiently gloomy!

I shall be back in Tokyo on the 11th of July. This letter will probably be sent from there. We have been warned not to expect much promptness from the Kamchatka post office—letters may take six months to reach their destination. But I can't help wishing I could surprise you with a letter bearing Russian stamps and perhaps an inscription in Russian which, on being translated, proves to be an assertion that this letter is travelling with breakneck speed to its destination.

I hope that your work on the new novel is progressing to your satisfaction. Perhaps you will know by this time if you have received the British prize for <u>The Great Fire</u>. You deserve every prize, and every acclamation, but I hope this will not keep you unduly from your work. My new work goes ahead slowly, hampered by imperfect vision. But I am otherwise well and in good spirits, so no doubt I shall soon get down to the actual writing.

[. . .]

All my best, dear Shirley. I shall write again from Japan.

As ever, Donald

NAPLES, OCTOBER 8, 2004

Dear Donald—on coming here, I found with delight your letter from ASUKA. A long time since I last had letter from a ship, or even knew anyone sailing on what we used to call "a liner". Your opening words, about passing in merciful fog through the island scenes of sixty-one years ago, brought to my mind the opening of part four of Auden's wonderful 1930s long poem "Letter to Lord Byron"—a brilliantly witty "take" on Byron's "Don Juan", and (like B's "DJ") not quite in <u>ottava rima</u>. If you don't yet know this poem of Auden's, I'll press it on you in January; when it will be the year 2005, with presumably all hell to pay. The looming election, three weeks away now, creates a dread, and suspense, felt around the world. Italy, having stuck far too long to its dwindling indulgence of America's policies, seems now unanimously horrified: if I haven't encountered a single soul who has a good word for Bush here, that may be, merely, because I don't have the privilege of knowing Berlusconi.

It's distressing to read about your eye strain. People "like us" need our eyes not only for pleasures and work but to feel ourselves truly alive at all. [. . .] Yes, I do indeed know the work of W G Sebald. A writing voice so deeply authentic, reminding me rather of Milosz. The first book of his that I read, <u>Emigrants</u>, was electrifying. As you say, too, the translator is beyond praise: Michael Hulse. I have almost no German, Francis spoke German, always claiming that he'd forgotten it entirely, but always equally prompt with it, and praised, when need arose. Whenever I hear <u>The Magic Flute</u>, I persuade myself I'll take German lessons—then the idea subsides. I'd like to have Michael Hulse as my teacher. [. . .]

Sebald's death, a mindless accident, was an example of the indifference and negligence of the gods: the most evil political figures live on without a scratch, and Rupert Murdoch flourishes in his seventies, while one's beloved friends and admired heroes disappear untimely, like Ivan or Steele Commager.

It would be marvellous to see Alaska's glaciers dripping into the sea, and I envy you the experience. But my time, or my expectations of it, compels choices these days, and I'd rather return to Venice. I'm hoping, in fact, to spend ten days, over Christmas and New Year on the island of Torcello out on the freezing lagoon of Venice, where Cipriani keeps six rooms over its fine little restaurant open for those holidays. Only thus could I hope to avoid Christmas in NYC, and to be truly "away" with my new work. I could fly NYC-Venice direct, and, leaving Venice, have a few days in Rome before returning to 10021. A retreat, indeed. Then home before your own arrival. A contrast with Kamchatka, and one that Chekov might applaud.

I hoped for those Russian stamps on your letter, but was pleased instead by the Japanese stamp announcing, in English, "International Letter-Writing Week", and by the pink flowers reminding me of the small cyclamens ready for gathering on Capri (which is beautiful in this warm and clear October), and of the dish that you brought me from Japan commemorating our Anacapri hours.

Thank you, dear Donald, for your warm words about my Great Fire. I didn't win either the Orange prize in Britain, or the Booker prize but I don't repine and have been lucky in any case. The generous prize I had in Australia came when I was in London as an Orange finalist, and I could not anyway have made the exhausting trip. However, "they" would like me to go there in June as a sort of follow-up, and I'm grateful, but fearful of mortgaging so much time and energy when I want to get on with new work. Meantime, I've been asked—and may accept—to the Hong Kong Literary Festival next March (a week in HK, a few days each in Shanghai and Beijing). This too would be exhausting; and emotional. I've, by choice, never returned to Asia. Now that my novel has been written, I feel I could make the journey this once. Everything will no doubt be unrecognisable, perhaps mercifully. But it seems unreasonable not to go, when all is being luxuriously arranged for me. The people arranging the HK festival are very keen to have articulate writers attend, in view of HK's predicament—to emphasise their window on the world's opinions, in the face of recent strictures.

I won't go to Japan yet, since in March—I think—you would not be there?

I fear that this present participation of mine in Letter-Writing Week may be the last straw, for a while, for your recovering sight. I'm at our Posillipo place, it is mild evening, absolutely silent except for the scratching of this pen. On the 20th of this month, Francis will have been dead for ten years. In our familiar rooms, he is everywhere. But also, of course, nowhere. All the familiar books, tables, plates, the familiar Vesuvius—all have outlasted his presence. How unyielding it is, this loss and absence. Auden (again) wrote that human beings are peculiarly afflicted by having the knowledge of our own mortality; while animals and nature need not reflect on it. Sonnets of Shakespeare also full of this reflection, and Keats . . .

I return to New York, on 7 November, with immediate roster of book-associated appointments—Chicago, Texas, Katonah . . . But then, I think, a reprieve; and Torcello . . . Can we dine together at the Academy on your return? I hope so. Thank you for such a precious letter. My great good wishes for your new work—perhaps now nearing completion? My greetings to Shiro, always. With all affection—Shirley

PS: I wonder, does Japanese have a second-person intimate form of address? (eg "tu"), or is this incorporated into the context of speech?

TOKYO, JULY 10, 2005

Dear Shirley,

I imagine that you will have returned to New York by now. That thought makes me wish I had not decided to remain in Japan in August. Perhaps I may yet change my mind, but I have been extremely busy with things that are more easily done here. One new experience for me is getting together all the illustrations for my new book on the painter Watanabe Kazan. I now have most of the needed color slides, but not all the permissions. In addition, I am told that transparencies reproduce better than slides. I have no idea of the difference between the two, but I am reluctant to start at the beginning again, getting transparencies instead of slides. Despite this, if all goes well, it should be an attractive book and will be the first in any European language to treat an important painter.

No doubt you are still struggling with the piles of letters that have accumulated, but perhaps you were able in the quieter surroundings of Capri to dispose of the urgent ones. My situation at the moment is quite the opposite. I long for letters from editors, museum people, prospective donors of funds and so on, usually restraining my impatience by telling myself that the people in question have other things to do than calm my nerves.

The voyage to the north was enjoyable, though there was still snow (in June) on the hills and occasionally the level ground in Norway and Iceland. Iceland at first was a great disappointment. Because of the many volcanoes much of the island (at least what I saw of it) is covered with lava. The view from my hotel window was bleak, a wasteland. The attraction of this hotel was the nearness of a hot spring that forms a considerable lake. One shivers in the cold until one gets into the warm water, and there one can gaze at the volcanoes that have made the hot spring possible. This probably does not sound very attractive to you, but to a Japanese this is heaven itself.

The people of Iceland are unusually pleasant. When one asks directions of a shopkeeper he or she is likely to walk with one, at least part of the way. At the airport, just before my plane took off for New York, I bought a copy of Independent People by Halldor Laxness. I remembered that he had won the Nobel Prize many years ago, but I had never read a word. The book is not the kind I like best. It gives much attention to sheep and there are many graphic descriptions of the interior of peasants' huts. But this is definitely a major work, whether I enjoy or not. I still haven't finished reading it, but I read a little when I feel up to it.

I am also reading a book called <u>Decadence</u> by Richard Gilman. Probably you have already read it. You read everything. But if you haven't, it is the kind of book you would enjoy. Gilman traces the meaning and uses of the word in many countries. I feel somewhat frustrated that there are no footnotes giving Gilman's sources but I have confidence in him.

It is now the rainy season. Most people dislike it, but it is relatively cool, and anything is better than the torrid heat of summer. I'm going to the Nō this afternoon. This will be my third time in a week. I didn't plan this; I just happened to be given a ticket by an acquaintance or actor. Last night was particularly moving. The performance was by candlelight. The high point was the entrance of the ghost. It must have taken him more than ten minutes to walk perhaps twenty yards. Not only was the pace extremely slow but it was accompanied by the harsh notes of the Nō flute, the whole suggesting how difficult and how painful it was for a ghost to return to this world.

I hope that, wherever you are, you are enjoying your work and your friends.

Best wishes as always, Donald

POSTCARD, NEW YORK, DECEMBER 7, 2005

(Fateful 7th Dec . . .)

Dear Donald—It seems, and is, long since we were in touch; and this greeting for Christmas and the impenetrable New Year is also to say how much I look forward to your 10 January arrival, and to a prompt reunion, if that is possible for you. I will myself then be recently back in New York from Venice and Torcello, where I am shamelessly returning for Christmas and New Year. We have much to catch up on—your new book—and our respective travels—New York is very cold and extremely busy. There are beautiful exhibitions, and our friends appear to thrive. I have nice times and am aware of being very lucky (Here I make the Sign against the Evil Eye . . .), but shall be glad to see Rome again, on my return journey to New York in the New Year. With all good wishes and all affection—Shirley.

TOKYO, JULY 26, 2006

Dear Shirley,

[…]

After we last met I once again was a passenger aboard the Japanese cruise ship Asuka. This time I joined the ship in Tallinn, Estonia, flying from New York by way of Amsterdam. The taxi ride from the airport was the worst possible introduction to Tallinn. The buildings were all of grey concrete, Soviet style, and there was the gloomy atmosphere typical of the old Soviet world. On top of that, I was outrageously overcharged by the taxi driver. I felt I had made a terrible mistake in opting for Tallinn as the point to join the Asuka. Looking from my hotel window, however, I could see a church steeple, and though I was exhausted from the overnight flight, I decided to make my way to the church. I walked with the steeple in sight until I passed through the great, turreted walls of the old city. Once inside, it was a different and enchanting world. I suppose that poverty had kept people from modifying the buildings in the interests of convenience and modernity, but it was a delight to walk along streets almost as silent as those in Venice. There were, of course, tourists, and shops selling amber jewelry and woolen hats for the tourists, but the architecture did not lie. I was sorry to leave after two days.

Next, the Asuka went to St Petersburg. I had visited it briefly under its old name Leningrad in the 1960s, but although there seem to be no new buildings, the place is totally changed. The city is a marvel. I can't remember if you have visited. If not, it would be worth making a special trip (vaut le détour). The Hermitage is magnificent, both as a building and as the repository of an incredible collection of paintings.

[…]

The journey aboard the Asuka ended for me, though not for the rest of the passengers who were on a round-the-world cruise, in Quebec. I had once before visited the city and had been disappointed, but this time I was delighted with this French city in Canada. I suppose the hotel made a great difference. The first time it was a dreary place, but this it was delightful.

From Quebec I flew to New York and had a few days there before flying to Tokyo. Here I have resumed my life, quite unlike my life in New York. I am already weary of giving lectures, and my stay has only begun. I'm publishing in a Japanese newspaper a kind of autobiography. When I was first approached by an editor of the newspaper I said that I had already twice published an autobiography and I wasn't sure I could find new information. She said quite politely that the two previous autobiographies had been published in books that had sold, at most, ten thousand copies, but the newspaper reached millions of readers. I hadn't much hope of success, but the series (an episode appears each Saturday) has attracted surprising attention. It is so easy to write that I suspect it can't be very good, but it is an agreeable experience at the age of eighty-four.

I hope that everything goes well with you and that you have had the time to work on your new book. I would be happy to hear from you if ever the demands on your time let up.

As ever, Donald

NEW YORK, DECEMBER 19, 2006

Dear Donald—

It is midnight, and I am packing for departure tomorrow to Rome— whence I'll be going on to Naples and Capri; returning to New York on 13 January. I look forward so much to seeing you then, and learning, among other things, how your new work is progressing. I am taking my own ms and a congenial book or two to Italy, hoping to resume my work after constant interruptions of appeals, demands, TASKS, that are increasingly encroaching on my life. I come to feel that brutality (on my part) is the only solution . . .

New York is frenzied with Christmas chaos. I enjoy seeing friends, hearing music, but the atmosphere of a crazy beehive is distracting. Otherwise, all is well privately, even while all is ill with the world; and I look forward to seeing Italy come up in the dawn the day after tomorrow.

If, as I hope, you will be attending the Academy meeting on the 17th, can we possibly sit together? How nice it will be to see you again.

With apologies for silence, with warmest thanks for your kind letter. With all affection—Shirley.

TOKYO, AUGUST 14, 2007

Dear Shirley,

It has been a very long time since I heard from you (and since I last wrote). I seem to have lost any sense of time ever since I had my accident. When Dr Deland said, "come back in six weeks" it seemed like a small eternity, but the time passed somehow. After the stated six weeks, the cast was removed, only to be replaced with a heavier one. This time I was told to come back in five weeks. Finally, I decided I would go to Japan. A new book was to appear, and it was desirable that I be present to help with the publicity. I went back to Dr Deland who said this time the cast could be replaced by a removable boot.

After reaching Tokyo I went to a good hospital where my foot was once again X rayed. I was told to come back in a month. Then, on the 8th of August, I saw the doctor. He informed me that the bone had not yet healed. "It will be a long process," he said. But he also said that I need not wear the boot any longer, and that I should go about my daily tasks normally, without worrying too much about the foot. And that is where I am now.

It has been four months since the accident. In retrospect, it seems like a period of undifferentiated, rather depressing time. But I've come to realize that I was lucky. Edward Seidensticker, a distinguished translator of Japanese, had a similar accident at almost the same time—going down a flight of stairs in Tokyo. He hit his head in falling, and has not regained consciousness after four months. That could have happened to me. I was also lucky in that Shiro so devotedly obtained food and everything else I needed. I cannot imagine how I would have survived otherwise, though I suppose that I could have hired someone.

I was lucky also in another way. I have been going over the notes I took on my readings while my leg was still in a cast. It is clear to me now that if I had been leading a normal life—making friends, going to concerts, visiting museums and so on—I could not have accomplished so much. I now have enough material for a book on Japanese writers during wartime and immediately afterwards. My problem is that I still have not thought of how to use the material, what kind of structure the book should have. No doubt this will come eventually.

This has been a terribly hot summer in Tokyo, but terribly hot summers are nothing new in Tokyo. As a lingering effect of my injury in the period of enforced seclusion, I find I am able to spend days happily with my work in an air-conditioned room without going out. No doubt I will feel differently when my foot has healed.

I am not quite undisturbed. Next year is officially the thousandth since the composition of <u>The Tale of Genji</u>, and preparations are already underway. Today two people came to verify I would give a lecture in November and another man telephoned about a lecture in December. I do not relish these lectures. Although <u>The Tale of Genji</u>

merits of celebration, the purpose of the events is probably to attract even greater crowds of tourists to Kyoto.

The one thing I miss most in my present life is conversation. How I would love to have a conversation with you! I have friends here and I am grateful to them for their many kindnesses, but I missed the pleasure of talking with old friends about things that matter to us.

I hope that you are well and that your work is proceeding to your satisfaction. I shall be back in New York on the tenth of January. I hope that you are there at that time.

As ever, Donald

TOKYO, OCTOBER 21, 2007

Dear Shirley,

When I wrote you in August I said we had not been in touch in a very long time. Now two additional months have passed without word from you. I hope that you have been well and that you haven't written simply because you haven't had the time.

[. . .]

I have managed to start a new book, on the diaries kept by Japanese writers during the war years.[4] I knew several of the writers, one of them very well. It has therefore come as a shock when I find him expressing a sense of relief and even joy that war has at last come, ending the prolonged tension and sweeping away the clouds of British and American culture. Now the radiant sunlight of Asia will shine unhindered. Another man, a quiet, amusing man who looked as if he might have devoted his life to the study of Tristram Shandy, revealed that his great hero was Hitler. Of course, he did not know what we know about Hitler's crimes, but still.

These are not the only voices. A professor of French at Tokyo University kept his diary in French so that the police would not be able to read it, and in it he expressed profound dismay with the terrible war into which the militarists had drawn their country. Another diarist attacked his countrymen for their inability to understand what was going on around them, contrasting their cruelty towards prisoners with the decency of Japan's enemies.

I still don't know how to present this new knowledge. Perhaps it will not be as exciting to other people as to myself, but I keep going back to the four war years I experienced, unlike any other period of my life.

I don't even know where you are now, but I shall send this letter to New York and hope that it reaches you.

As ever, Donald

TOKYO, JULY 21, 2008

Dear Shirley,

It will soon be a month since I arrived in Japan. What have I been doing? The day after I arrived I was obliged to attend a party at the Irish embassy in honor of an Irish friend who has recently published a volume of translations of mediaeval Japanese poetry. Of course, I was glad to go, but my talk on this occasion was not one of my most stimulating. The next day I had a dialogue with a famous Kabuki actor. This was enjoyable, though I grew steadily more sleepy. Every day there has been something to occupy me. Most of these engagements are in some way agreeable, but I find it very difficult to do my own work or even to write letters.

The most time-consuming activity lies ahead. I may have mentioned to you that the thousandth anniversary of the writing of

<u>The Tale of Genji</u> will be celebrated this year. I have been asked to deliver lectures on the work all over the country. I have attempted to refuse, laying stress on my great age, but the people who ask for the lectures are almost always so unhappy when I refuse that, sooner or later, I am persuaded. I have never learned the pronunciation of the word NO.

Despite my silence, I often think of you and wonder if the injury you suffered has now completely healed. It looks as if I shall be going to Venice in September, but everything is extremely vague. A foundation, which apparently has a building of its own on the island of San Giorgio, has invited me, among a dozen others. They expect me to give a lecture on <u>The Tale of Genji</u>, to last no longer than thirty minutes. This seems easy, but (if there were nothing else to detain me in Italy) it would be rather strange to invite someone all the way from Japan to talk for thirty minutes, and this possibly includes a ten minute introduction. But, of course, there is much to detain me (and anyone else) in Italy. By a curious coincidence, there is to be a gathering of scholars of Japan in Lecce about the same time. I have not been invited, possibly because I am considered too old, but it would be delightful to spend time in Lecce, a city I visited for one day some years ago.

I hope very much to see you in Italy. I expect to have about a week on my own, from about the tenth to the seventeenth of September.

All my best to you, dear Shirley.
As ever, Donald

ACKNOWLEDGMENTS

My work on this book has been supported by an Australian Research Council Discovery Project grant (DP230101797) and by a period of sabbatical leave granted by the School of the Arts & Media, Faculty of Art & Design, University of New South Wales, Sydney.

I would like to thank Jennifer Crewe for her enthusiasm for the project, and the editorial and production team at Columbia University Press for their impeccable work on the manuscript. Finally I would like formally to thank the estate of Donald Keene for permission to publish Keene's letters, and The Trustees of the New York Society Library for their permission to publish Hazzard's letters.

NOTES

SOURCES

In the introduction and notes, I have provided full citations of published sources in a source's first note; subsequent references have a short-form citation. The notes provide a full bibliography of published and unpublished sources used in the book.

Shirley Hazzard and Donald Keene's correspondence is held in the Shirley Hazzard Papers 1920–2016, Rare Book and Manuscript Library, Columbia University Libraries, New York.

INTRODUCTION

1. Donald Keene, "In Memoriam: Ivan Morris, 1925–1965," *Monumenta Nipponica* (Winter 1976): 416.
2. Donald Keene, *Meeting with Japan* (Tokyo: Gakusiesha, 1978), 1.
3. Hazzard to Keene, December 29, 1980.
4. Donald Keene, *On Familiar Terms: A Journey Across Cultures* (New York: Kodansha, 1994), 132.
5. Jan Garrett, "The Transits of Hazzard," *Look and Listen* (November 1984): 39.
6. Trish Evans, "Shirley's 'Transit' Is a Rare Event," *Weekend Australian*, November 29–30, 1980, 13.
7. Lucy Latané Gordan and T. M. Pasca, "Shirley Hazzard: Back to Basics," *Wilson Library Bulletin* 65 no. 3 (November 1980): 45.

8. Shirley Hazzard, "Bread and Circuses: Thought and Language in Decline," *Sydney Papers* 9 no. 4 (1997): 28.

9. Jay Parini spoke on a panel called "Shirley Hazzard: Literary Icon" at the New York Society Library, September 7, 2012. Recording at https://www.nysoclib.org/events/shirley-hazzard-literary-icon.

10. Michael Hofmann, "Citizen of Nowhere," *Times Literary Supplement*, January 20, 2012, https://www.the-tls.co.uk/articles/shirley-hazzard-brigitta-olubas-book-review-michael-hofmann/.

11. Shirley Hazzard to Elizabeth Harrower, March 9, 1980, Papers of Elizabeth Harrower (1937–2005), National Library of Australia.

12. See Timothy Duffy, "The Gender of Letters," *New England Quarterly* 69 no. 1 (1996): 92.

13. Shirley Hazzard, "Lives Well Lived: Francis Steegmuller: Our Reading List," *New York Times*, January 1, 1995.

14. Roland Barthes, "Réquichot and His Body," in *The Responsibility of Forms* (Oxford: Blackwell, 1985), 230.

15. Jamie Katz, "Sensei and Sensibility," *Columbia College Today* (Winter 2011–2012): 30.

16. Katz, "Sensei and Sensibility," 30.

17. Donald Keene, "Living in Two Countries," in *The Blue-Eyed Tarōkaja: A Donald Keene Anthology*, ed. J. Thomas Rimer (New York: Columbia University Press, 1996), 284.

18. Donald Keene, "The New Generation of American Japanologists," in *The Blue-Eyed Tarōkaja: A Donald Keene Anthology*, ed. J. Thomas Rimer (New York: Columbia University Press, 1996), 80.

19. Keene, *On Familiar Terms*, 33.

20. Keene, *On Familiar Terms*, 193.

21. Donald Keene, *Chronicles of My Life: An American in the Heart of Japan* (New York: Columbia University Press, 2008), 24.

22. Keene, *Chronicles of My Life*, 22, 23, 36.

23. Keene, *On Familiar Terms*, 23.

24. Katz, "Sensei and Sensibility," 32.

25. Keene, *On Familiar Terms*, 23–24.

26. Donald Keene "The Eroica Symphony," in *The Blue-Eyed Tarōkaja: A Donald Keene Anthology*, ed. J. Thomas Rimer (New York: Columbia University Press, 1996), 13.

27. Keene, "The Eroica Symphony," 15.

28. Donald Keene, *Emperor of Japan: Meiji and His World, 1852–1912* (New York: Columbia University Press, 2002), xiii.

29. Donald Keene, *Yoshimasa and the Silver Pavilion: The Creation of the Soul of Japan* (New York: Columbia University Press, 2003) 166.

30. Keene, *Yoshimasa and the Silver Pavilion*, 9.

31. Keene, *On Familiar Terms*, 236.

32. Donald Keene, "Introduction," in Mishima Yukio, *Five Modern Nō Plays*, trans. Donald Keene (Tokyo: Charles E Tuttle Company, 1957), xi.

33. Keene, *On Familiar Terms*, 83.

34. Keene, *On Familiar Terms*, 273.

35. Keene, *On Familiar Terms*, 84.

36. Keene, *On Familiar Terms*, 95.

37. Keene, *On Familiar Terms*, 89–90.

38. Katz, "Sensei and Sensibility," 30.

39. Katz, "Sensei and Sensibility," 33.

40. Donald Keene, *Travellers of a Hundred Ages: The Japanese as Revealed Through 1,000 Years of Diaries* (New York: Henry Holt, 1989); Donald Keene, *Modern Japanese Diaries: The Japanese at Home and Abroad as Revealed Through Their Diaries* (New York: Henry Holt, 1995).

41. Martin Collcutt, "Review of *Travellers of a Hundred Ages: The Japanese as Revealed Through 1,000 Years of Diaries*" *Monumenta Nipponica* 45 no. 3 (Autumn 1990): 357.

42. Donald Keene, *So Lovely a Country Will Never Perish: Wartime Diaries of Japanese Writers* (New York: Columbia University Press, 2010), 5.

43. Keene, *So Lovely a Country*, 6.

44. Keene, *So Lovely a Country*, 4–5.

45. David Pilling, "Lunch with the FT: Donald Keene," *Financial Times* October 28, 2011 https://www.ft.com/content/9a0ebac8-00f5-11e1-8590 -00144feabdc0.

46. Takami Jun, diary entry for March 13, 1945, quoted in Keene, *So Lovely a Country*, 80.

47. Pilling, "Lunch with the FT."

48. Pilling, "Lunch with the FT."

49. Ken Moritsugu, "Scholar of Japan," *Business Insider*, December 30, 2015, n.p.

50. Quoted in Ben Dooley, "Donald Keene, Famed Translator of Japanese Literature, Dies at 96," *New York Times*, February 24, 2019, D6.

1. 1977–1986

1. Donald Keene, "The Barren Years: Japanese War Literature," *Monumenta Nipponica* 33, no.1 (Spring 1978): 67–112.

2. Edita Morris, mother of Ivan Morris.

3. Annalita Marsili Alexander had been engaged to Ivan Morris at the time of his death.

4. Donald Keene, *Meeting with Japan* (Tokyo: Gakuseisha, 1978).

5. Mishima Yukio was one of the most significant novelists of the twentieth century, admired in Japan and internationally for the range and quality of his writing and also for having taken his own life by sepukku. He was a good friend of Keene's and Keene translated some of Mishima's work.

6. Donald Keene, *Dawn to the West* (New York: Holt, Rhinehart and Winston, 1984).

7. Keene provides an account of the invitation in both his memoirs: *On Familiar Terms: A Journey Across Cultures* (New York: Kodansha International, 1994), and *Chronicles of My Life: An American in the Heart of Japan* (New York: Columbia University Press, 2008). In the first of these memoirs, he comments that he thought the intention behind the invitation was "to make the newspaper more international." Donald Keene, *On Familiar Terms: A Journey Across Cultures* (New York: Kodansha International, 1994), 275.

8. Hazzard had been invited to present the prestigious annual "Boyer Lectures" for the Australian Broadcasting Commission.

9. Hazzard published a number of articles critical of the United Nations, where she had worked in the early 1950s. In 1980 she published an article implying that then-Secretary General Kurt Waldheim had falsified his wartime records to conceal his connection with the Nazis, and the story had broken more widely in 1986, while Waldheim was seeking to be elected president of Austria. A fuller account is provided in Brigitta Olubas, *Shirley Hazzard: A Writing Life* (New York: Farrar, Straus & Giroux, 2022).

10. Lily Aprile was a longtime close friend of Hazzard's living in Naples. Keene met her whenever he visited Hazzard there.

11. It was Joseph Stalin who used the term, not Adolf Hitler.

2. 1987–1997

1. Donald Keene, *Travelers of a Hundred Ages* (New York: Henry Holt, 1989).
2. Hazzard's friend, Naples historian Carlo Knight.
3. The Naples historian Carlo Knight was a good friend of Hazzard's. The occasion was the marriage of his daughter Ella.
4. Hazzard published two essays on Waldheim in 1989: "Reflections: Breaking Faith," in the *New Yorker*, September 25, 63–99, and in the *New Yorker* of October 2, 74–96. These essays were later expanded and published in book form as *Countenance of Truth: The United Nations and the Waldheim Case* (New York: Viking, 1990)
5. Kōbō Abe, *Three Plays*, trans. Donald Keene (New York: Columbia University Press, 1993).
6. Francis Steegmuller died October 20, 1994.
7. The postcard shows a painting by Frans Post, "Brazilian Landscape with a Worker's House (detail) 1655."

3. 1997–2008

1. Makoto Oda, *The Breaking Jewel*, trans. Donald Keene (New York: Columbia University Press, 2003).
2. Donald Keene, *Yoshimasa and the Silver Pavilion: The Creation of the Soul of Japan* (New York: Columbia University Press, 2003).
3. Donald Keene, *Frog in the Well: Portraits of Japan by Watanabe Kazan 1793–1841* (New York: Columbia University Press, 2006).
4. Donald Keene, *So Lovely a Country Will Never Perish: Wartime Diaries of Japanese Writers* (New York: Columbia University Press, 2010).

GPSR Authorized Representative: Easy Access System Europe, Mustamäe tee
50, 10621 Tallinn, Estonia, gpsr.requests@easproject.com

www.ingramcontent.com/pod-product-compliance
Lightning Source LLC
Chambersburg PA
CBHW031040310726
48969CB00007B/2051